## Management Extra

# POSITIVE WORKING RELATIONSHIPS

Management Extra

# POSITIVE WORKING RELATIONSHIPS

ELSEVIER

eLEARN

Pergamon
*Flexible*
Learning

AMSTERDAM • BOSTON • HEIDELBERG • LONDON • NEW YORK • OXFORD • PARIS •
SAN DIEGO • SAN FRANCISCO • SINGAPORE • SYDNEY • TOKYO

Elsevier Butterworth-Heinemann
Linacre House, Jordan Hill, Oxford OX2 8DP
30 Corporate Drive, Burlington, MA 01803

First published 2005

**British Library Cataloguing in Publication Data**
A catalogue record for this book is available from the British Library

**Library of Congress Cataloguing in Publication Data**
A catalogue record for this book is available from the Library of Congress

ISBN 0 7506 6678 1

For information on all Elsevier Butterworth-Heinemann publications
visit our website at www.books.elsevier.com

Printed and bound in Italy

# Contents

## Activities

# Figures

# Tables

# Series preface

*'I hear I forget
I see I remember
I do I understand'*

Galileo

Management Extra is designed to help you put ideas into practice. Each book in the series is full of thought-provoking ideas, examples and theories to help you understand the key management concepts of our time. There are also activities to help you see how the concepts work in practice.

The text and activities are organised into bite-sized themes or topics. You may want to review a theme at a time, concentrate on gaining understanding through the text or focus on the activities whilst dipping into the text for reference.

The activities are varied. Some are work-based, asking you to consider changing, developing and extending your current practice. Others ask you to reflect on new ideas, check your understanding or assess the application of concepts in different contexts. The activities will give you a valuable opportunity to practise various techniques in a safe environment.

And, finally, exploring and sharing your ideas with others can be very valuable in making the most of this resource.

More information on using this book as part of a course or programme of learning is available on the Management Extra website.

www.managementextra.co.uk

# Building productive relationships at work

*He was an experienced software designer, presenting the results of weeks of work to his boss. He had worked long days and felt proud of his specification. As he finished his presentation, the Development Director turned to him and said sarcastically 'So, this is it – do you expect me to approve this?'*

*Embarrassed and deflated, the designer stared glumly back. The phone rang and the Development Director was called away for the rest of the week. The designer was obsessed with his boss's remarks and totally unable to concentrate. By the end of the week, he had convinced himself he would never be trusted with another important project and that his only option was to find a new job.*

*The following week, he met with the Director again. 'I need to understand what was so wrong with the specification.' The Director apologised. He had been meaning to voice his concerns about the project for a couple of weeks but had been too busy.*

It takes just one incident to damage the trust between people. Trust is a vital ingredient in any productive relationship. To gain it, there has to be openness and honesty and this only happens if we communicate effectively and behave in a way that represents our true feelings and needs.

We start this book by looking at the principles of communication and assertive behaviour. Applying these principles enables openness and honesty to be brought into a relationship and paves the way for more successful working relationships. We then look at how you can build better working relationships by using these skills in three areas of your work as a manager: negotiations, meetings and conflict management.

Your objectives are to:

◆ Become a more effective communicator

◆ Master your ability to think and behave assertively in difficult situations

◆ Develop your skills for leading and participating in meetings

◆ Find out how to negotiate win-win solutions

◆ Improve your ability to manage conflicts of interest and disagreements.

# 1 Communicating to connect

There are a whole host of reasons to study communication:

◆ Communication continues to be one of the most frequently cited problems in organisations

◆ Almost no one works alone and the job of most managers in particular involves interacting with people

◆ New communication technologies have changed the way that we communicate

◆ Our society and working environment is increasingly diverse and multicultural and this poses new communication challenges.

Communication is a vital but complex leadership skill central to your ability to form relationships and to generate commitment, co-operation and enthusiasm.

In this theme, you will:

◆ **Explore models of effective interpersonal communication**

◆ **Identify factors that influence organisational communication**

◆ **Recognise the main barriers to effective communication**

◆ **Discover six skills for improving your verbal communication.**

> **Conversation: a competitive sport in which the first person to draw breath is declared the listener.**

## What is communication?

Communication in organisations is full of contradictions. On the one hand, everyone agrees that it is vitally important – the lifeblood of the organisation. As early as 1916, Henri Fayol, the French engineer, put communication at the centre of his 'wheel of management activities'. Ask any group of employees what matters most to them and you will almost certainly find 'good communication' high on the list.

On the other hand, communication is one of the things that organisations most often get wrong. Charles Handy, in *Understanding Organisations* (1993), gives a list of studies showing how often communication fails to get through. Here are just two examples:

> **Communication is one of the things that organisations most often get wrong.**

◆ A study of communication in companies found that information communicated by top management was only remembered by one in five people on the shop floor

♦ In another case study, while 95 per cent of supervisors felt they understood the problems of the people in their teams well, just 35 per cent of their team members agreed.

So, it is clearly important for managers to be good communicators, and to understand the process well. But what exactly is communication?

In their book *Understanding Information* (1990), Jonathon Liebenau and James Backhouse define communication as follows:

> Communication is a process which involves at least two parties. This process can be characterised as a set of activities involving a sender with intentions to convey, a medium or channel for carrying signals, and a receiver who has the ability to interpret those signals.

Source: *Liebenau and Backhouse* (1990)

Within this broad definition it is important to distinguish between:

♦ spoken and written communication

♦ verbal and non-verbal communication

♦ formal and informal communication.

## Spoken and written communication

The first key distinction is between spoken communication – where we speak and listen – and written communication – where we write and read.

As Stephen Covey comments, managers spend many hours a day speaking, listening, reading and writing:

> The ability to do them well is absolutely critical to your effectiveness.

Source: *Covey* (1992)

Covey highlights the skills of listening as especially important. He points out that we all spend a lot of time at school learning to read, write and speak, but much less learning to listen and in practice it is listening skills that can be especially important to managers.

It is not only these skills that are crucial for a manager; we also need to be able to decide when spoken or written communication is more appropriate.

### Verbal and non-verbal communication

The second key distinction is between verbal and non-verbal communication:

◆ Verbal communication is the words that we say or write down when we communicate

◆ Non-verbal communication is the messages we convey without words by our tone of voice, our expressions, the gestures we make and other aspects of our 'body language', such as posture.

You will consider the impact of non-verbal cues when you look at verbal communication skills later in this book.

### Formal and informal communication

The third key distinction is between formal and informal communication:

◆ Formal communication is the communication up, down and along the hierarchy of the organisation. It includes communication with your boss, with your team and the colleagues with whom you are expected to communicate using reports, letters, memos, meetings, etc.

◆ Informal communication, by contrast, includes the rumours that race round organisations, the informal networks between friends and the grapevine.

The conventions we use for communicating vary. We will use very different conventions for a formal, written letter than for an informal conversation. We may use different words, different kinds of sentence, different forms of address, and so on.

These conventions evolve as communication evolves. The growth of e-mail is one fascinating example of this: while e-mails are a written form of communication and are often used in formal contexts, they often use the conventions of informal, spoken communication. In this they may both reflect a change towards less formal conventions at work, and help to drive this change.

## Some key aspects of communication

When you need to communicate with other people, there are a number of key aspects to consider:

◆ Purpose – first consider what you want to achieve by the communication. How do you want the receiver to react? What do you want them to do or think?

◆ Audience – it is equally vital to consider who you are communicating to. This will have an impact on what you say and how you say it – you will need to use terminology they understand, and adopt a style and level of formality appropriate to them.

◆ Medium – you also need to consider how you will put your message across, and select an appropriate medium – whether one-to-one, by telephone, in a group or meeting, by letter or e-mail, and so on.

◆ Context – equally important is the context within which communication takes place – and in particular the level of trust and co-operation between people.

**The higher the level of trust and co-operation, the better the communication.**

### The importance of trust and co-operation to communication

Stephen Covey uses the diagram shown in Figure 1.1 to underline the importance of trust and co-operation for communication.

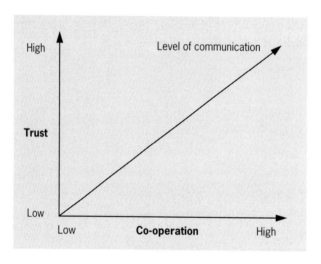

**Figure 1.1** *Trust and co-operation in communication*          Source: *Covey* (1992)

## Communication in new organisations

The changes in organisations in recent years have had two important ramifications for communication. Firstly, developments such as Total Quality and Investors in People (IIP), with their emphasis on people, have put the role of communication even more firmly at the centre of an organisation. Secondly, changes in organisations have affected how communication takes place. In particular:

◆ The tendency towards flatter, less hierarchical organisations has had a significant impact on communication within organisations. There are fewer layers to communicate across and, in some organisations at least, less formality.

◆ The increasing use of teamworking and project organisation calls for greater collaborative skills.

◆ The trend towards keeping core operations in-house and outsourcing other services has led to new patterns of communication between customers and suppliers.

◆ New media – in particular e-mail but also company intranets and video conferencing facilities – have had an important impact on communication. In many cases communication is now more direct and immediate.

One result of these changes is that there is now often greater emphasis on spoken communication than on written communication.

## Activity 1
## Examine communication in your organisation

### Objective

Use this activity to take an overview of communication in your organisation.

### Task

1 Read each of the statements in the following table. The statements begin with communication in your team, and then widen out to the broader organisation and its relationships with the outside world.

2 Decide whether each statement is always true, sometimes true, sometimes untrue or always untrue, and tick the appropriate box.

| Statement | Always true | Sometimes true | Sometimes untrue | Always untrue |
|---|---|---|---|---|
| I believe that communication is important for my team | ☐ | ☐ | ☐ | ☐ |
| I put my trust in the people in my team | ☐ | ☐ | ☐ | ☐ |
| People in my team talk to me when they have a problem | ☐ | ☐ | ☐ | ☐ |
| I can talk to my manager when I have a problem | ☐ | ☐ | ☐ | ☐ |
| My manager communicates openly with me | ☐ | ☐ | ☐ | ☐ |
| We communicate openly with other teams in the organisation | ☐ | ☐ | ☐ | ☐ |
| Other teams in the organisation communicate openly with us | ☐ | ☐ | ☐ | ☐ |
| Senior managers communicate effectively with staff | ☐ | ☐ | ☐ | ☐ |
| Staff can raise problems and concerns with senior managers | ☐ | ☐ | ☐ | ☐ |
| The organisation communicates effectively with customers | ☐ | ☐ | ☐ | ☐ |
| The organisation communicates effectively with suppliers | ☐ | ☐ | ☐ | ☐ |
| The organisation presents a coherent image to the outside world | ☐ | ☐ | ☐ | ☐ |

## Feedback

Reflect on which boxes you have ticked. Ticks in the 'true' boxes on the left-hand side suggest an atmosphere of trust and openness; those in the right-hand 'untrue' boxes suggest a climate of distrust and insularity.

What does this tell you about:

◆ communication within your team?

◆ communication between your team and other parts of the organisation?

◆ the overall climate of communication in the organisation?

◆ the way your organisation communicates with the outside world?

*Make a note of any ideas you have for improvement*

## Models of the communication process

Given the importance of communication to organisations, it is perhaps not surprising that a large number of writers have discussed the subject. In particular, some writers have provided models of the communication process which may help you to develop your understanding of your interactions with other people and will therefore be relevant to other topics in this book. This section describes some of the more important models and suggests some ways in which they may be useful in your work.

### Return to sender? – Coding and decoding

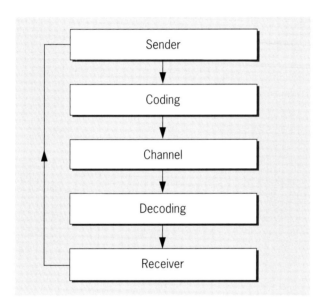

**Figure 1.2** *Sending and receiving information*

Source: *Liebenau and Backhouse* (1990)

The first model of communication focuses very much on the process itself, and how a message is transmitted from sender to receiver (see Figure 1.2). Within this model a number of things must happen if communication is to take place:

- ◆ Firstly, there must be a sender – the person who does the communicating – who sends the message.
- ◆ Secondly, there must be a receiver – the person the sender wishes to communicate to – who will receive the message.
- ◆ The sender must choose a channel or medium to send their message – this could be face to face, via letter or e-mail, over the phone, and so on.
- ◆ The sender must also choose a 'code' in which to send the message – coding. This is a crucial part of the process – the sender must choose the language and words that the receiver will understand, but also needs to observe other conventions, such as body language.

♦ Finally, the receiver must be able to decode the message – to interpret and understand it.

Problems with communication can happen at any stage in the process:

♦ If the sender chooses inappropriate coding – for example, complex terminology or inappropriate slang – the message will not make sense to the receiver

♦ The message could get lost or jumbled in the channel – a letter may go to the wrong address, the attachment to an e-mail may become unreadable, spoken words may be hard to hear in a crowded room or railway carriage

♦ The receiver may not decode the message correctly – they may misread it or hear something incorrectly, or they may misunderstand a gesture or expression.

The value of this model to you as a manager is in helping you to think through the whole process and the points where things can go wrong in order to plan your communication more effectively. In thinking about communication, it is also helpful to consider the idea of feedback – the sender does not know the message has been received as intended until they get feedback or some other response.

## Transactional analysis

A very different way of looking at communication comes from the world of psychotherapy. Transactional analysis – often shortened to TA – was developed by Eric Berne and draws extensively on the ideas of the father of psychotherapy, Sigmund Freud.

**Games People Play**

In his book *Games People Play* (1968) Berne argued that there are three different parts of any person's personality – what Berne calls 'ego states' – and each shows itself in different ways of thinking, feeling and acting. They are:

♦ The Parent – these are the behaviours, thoughts and feelings drawn from parents or parent figures. The 'Critical' Parent shows prejudices and makes judgements; the 'Nurturing' Parent is caring and protective.

♦ The Adult – the Adult is able to look at things objectively, to analyse, reflect and question what is happening.

♦ The Child – these are the behaviours, thoughts and feelings replayed from childhood. The 'Natural' Child behaves spontaneously, showing spontaneity, feelings and creativity; the 'Adapted' Child behaves as the Parent expects them to behave, showing compliance or complaining.

Source: *Berne* (1968)

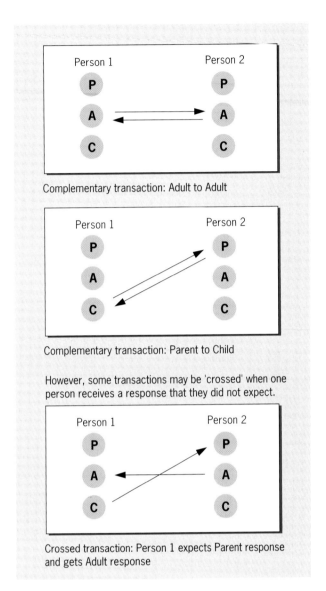

**Figure 1.3** *Transactional analysis*

Source: *Berne* (1968) and *Guirdham* (1995)

We have all had parents/parent figures and experience of childhood and adulthood, and we may all adopt one or other of these states in any social interaction. Berne argues that certain states are complementary – in particular Adult to Adult and Parent to Child (see Figure 1.3).

The ideas of transactional analysis can be invaluable to managers. As Maureen Guirdham (1995) comments, it is a 'way of increasing awareness both of self and of communications'. You can reflect on how you are behaving in a particular social interaction, and you can also observe other people's behaviours and whether each of you is adopting a Parent, Child or Adult ego state, and the impact this has on communication.

## The systems approach

Both the models we have described so far look principally at communication between individuals. The next two models focus more on communication within the wider organisation. The first is the systems approach shown in Figure 1.4.

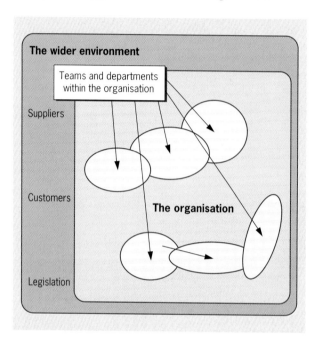

**Figure 1.4** *The organisation as an open system*

The systems approach gives a model for analysing communication within and beyond the organisation. You can analyse who needs to communicate with whom, how effectively they communicate, and so on. People developing computer systems for organisations often draw on the systems model.

## Codification and diffusion

The ideas contained in the systems approach help us to picture the patterns of communication within an organisation, and between an organisation and the wider environment. However, they give us limited information about the nature of the communication itself.

In recent years, we have become increasingly aware of the importance of cultures within organisations. The culture can be defined as the set of values, norms and behaviours that are typical of the organisation – it is the way that people tend to think and act within the organisation.

**Max Boisot: Codification and diffusion**
Anthropologist Max Boisot uses the following matrix – what he calls the 'C-space' – to show how organisations codify and diffuse information. Here are some examples:

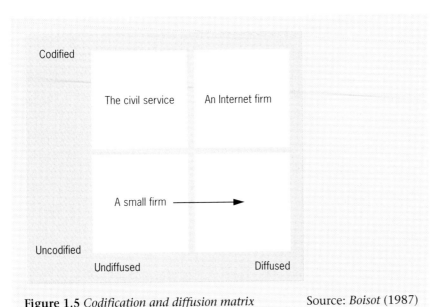

**Figure 1.5** *Codification and diffusion matrix*          Source: *Boisot* (1987)

In these examples, a small firm founded by a single person may tend to have uncodified knowledge, known only by the owner. This knowledge may become more diffused as the firm expands. By contrast, in a bureaucracy like the civil service, more information may be highly codified but still restricted to those 'in the know'. In a more open, networked organisation, such as a modern Internet company, more information, while still codified, may be more widely diffused among the staff.

Organisational culture has an important impact on communication. In his book *Information in Organisations: The Manager as Anthropologist* (1987), Boisot argues that different types of organisation have very different ways of communicating. Boisot suggests that it is possible to classify organisations according to how much they codify and diffuse information:

◆ Codification is the extent to which we use codes such as technical language in our communication. For example, a doctor has to decide whether to describe a condition to a patient in highly codified, medical language that is accurate but inaccessible to the patient, or whether to choose everyday words that may be less accurate but which the patient is more likely to understand.

◆ Diffusion is the extent to which the organisation shares or 'broadcasts' information. Information is undiffused if very few people have access to it; it is widely diffused if everyone has access to it.

You can examine communication in your own organisation using this model. Do people share information widely or do they hoard it for their own purposes? Do they dress it up in highly technical jargon or do they use clear English?

## Activity 2
### Examine the communication process

### Objective

Use this activity to examine the communication process.

### Task

Earlier in this section you looked at the following model of the communication process.

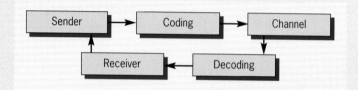

**Figure 1.6** *Sending and receiving information*

At each stage in this process things can go wrong, and one key task of the skilled communicator is to reduce the risks of this happening.

1  Identify a piece of information that you need to communicate over the next week. Choose something that is reasonably important, where it matters that you get the communication right. Note this down in the box provided.

2  What are the issues that you need to consider at each stage of the process? In particular, what could go wrong:

   ◆  when you, as sender, code the message?

   ◆  in the channel of communication you use?

   ◆  when the receiver decodes the message?

3  Plan what you can do to reduce the risks of things going wrong. Bear in mind the importance of building in opportunities for feedback.

4  Review how well the communication goes in practice.

*What you need to communicate:*

| Possible issues to consider | How to reduce the risks | What happens |
| --- | --- | --- |
| | | |

What you have learned from this:

## Barriers to communication

We are all well aware of the ways in which our intention to communicate can be blocked or the message distorted. You have probably experienced the distortion which occurs in 'Chinese whispers', where a sentence whispered from person to person becomes barely recognisable by the time it reaches the last person. This distortion occurs many times at work. The nature of organisational life and our own enthusiasm to leap to conclusions based on a few scraps of information means that this is normal. However, if we look at the way in which the communication process operates, we may be able to effect a few improvements or at least reduce the number of times that we finish up wasting our energies on miscommunication.

> Handy (1993) suggests that it is perhaps worth admiring the fact that any sensible communication takes place at all.

### Barriers at each stage of communication

One way of looking at barriers is to consider what may go wrong at each stage of the communication process. Remember the model that you looked at earlier for sending and receiving a message (Figure 1.2).

Guirdham (1995) develops this model by adding examples of possible sources of error for each stage in the communication, see Figure 1.7. Note that she calls the channel 'transmission', and splits it into two aspects: medium and environment.

The model shown in Figure 1.7 highlights a range of potential errors which can creep into the message between the sender having an idea in their mind and the receiver taking the message into their mind.

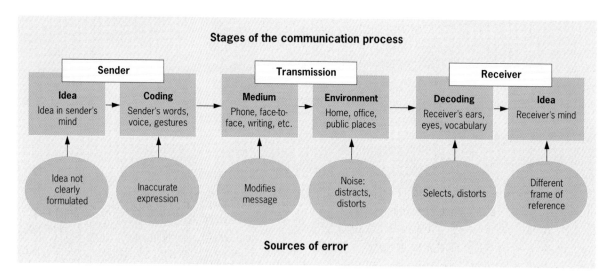

**Figure 1.7** *Sources of error at each stage in the communication process*

Source: *Adapted from Guirdham* (1995)

### Sender errors

The sender may not have formulated the message clearly in their own mind. For example, when going into a meeting you may know you have an objection to make, but not be too sure exactly what it is. The way the sender codes the message may give an inaccurate expression. For example, you may not use the best word to describe a feeling, or may use complex sentences in a report.

### Transmission errors

The medium used may modify the message. For example, using the phone precludes body language as part of the message.

The environment may distort the message. For example, a crackle on the phone line may mean that words are misheard.

### Receiver errors

Decoding may distort the message. For example, the receiver may hear 'the budget is a lie', rather than 'the budget is high'.

The receiver's perceptions may distort the message. For example, as an accountant the receiver may think that a the proposal is not viable, whereas the sender, who is a rural development officer, may feel that the social benefits of the proposal outweigh the financial costs.

In an ongoing communication, as the messages progress backwards and forwards between receiver and sender, the scope for errors increases. In a group situation, such as a meeting, where each participant has differing perceptions, the scope for errors increases even further. You may have witnessed this by comparing notes with colleagues after a meeting and finding you each have a different idea of what you think was agreed.

Failure to invite or give feedback is another major barrier. In a conversation, you need to periodically check your understanding to avoid 'miscommunication', which can happen even though both parties feel they are communicating well. You have much more scope to obtain feedback during verbal communications than written ones.

## Types of barrier

Sources of error in communications are not necessarily tied to specific stages in the communication process. For example, differing perceptions and assumptions can be held by both sender and receiver. So, another way to look at barriers is to consider the main types of barrier that can get in the way of the message being received and understood. Here are some examples:

> **Making your own perceptions clear and recognising those of others will help to achieve shared understanding.**

### Environment

The environment in which the communication takes place may contain physical or emotional barriers.

Physical barriers operate mainly in the transmission of the message. They include:

◆ interference: for example, distractions when holding a meeting in an open-plan office, noise of roadworks outside, not being able to see the slides during a presentation

◆ discomfort, which affects concentration: for example the room being too hot or too cold.

Emotional barriers, such as one person feeling very anxious, or strong emotions like anger in a meeting, can charge up the atmosphere and distort messages.

### Language

The language used is at the heart of the coding and decoding processes. If the language is unfamiliar to one of the parties, the message becomes cloudy.

A common language barrier is the use of jargon and abbreviations, for example scientific jargon or terms associated with a discipline such as finance or law. Sometimes people deliberately use jargon as a form of power over others who may not feel confident enough to question the terms used, but most of the time language barriers are quite unintentional.

Text messaging, as used on cellular phones, is an example of a language which is perfectly comprehensible to those in the know, yet double Dutch to those who do not use it.

**What does CBT mean to you?**
A trainer and a psychologist were considering how to update a training package on post-natal depression. The psychologist suggested CBT, and they talked for some time before the trainer realised that CBT could not be 'computer-based training'. On enquiring, she found that the psychologist was talking about 'cognitive behaviour therapy'!

## Culture

Managers working in the global market need to be aware of cultural differences, including:

◆ silence – more acceptable to Asians than to Europeans

◆ personal space – British and Americans require more than other cultures

◆ greeting habits – for example, in Spain, France, Italy and Latin America, male colleagues embrace, while the Japanese bow from a distance and always accompany introductions with visiting cards

◆ gestures – for example, pointing with a finger is considered rude in China, and shaking your head from side to side means 'yes' to Indians.

Guirdham (1995) says that to work with people of other cultures you must go deeper than this and be aware of ways of working; for example, Americans value straight-line logic and direct verbal interaction, whereas the Japanese value spiral logic and indirect verbal interaction. There are also many cultural differences within countries which you need to be aware of. For example, managers who have worked in both the private and public sectors notice their contrasting ways of working.

## Perceptions

Differing perceptions of the parties involved can form major barriers in communication. As the following list shows, there are very many ways in which perceptions can differ. Because perceptions are often 'invisible' and subconscious they frequently go undetected. In some cases perceptions are used in a deliberately manipulative way.

- ◆ **Meaning of words**, for example, 'dangerous' means different things to different people depending on the danger level they have experienced.

- ◆ **Stereotyping**, for example, having dealt with one PR person you assume they are all the same and make assumptions about them.

- ◆ **Jumping to conclusions** about what the person is going to say, so you hear what you expect to hear rather than what they say.

- ◆ **Unstated assumptions** – for example, we both know what we are talking about, we need to agree, we know each other's views, we shouldn't let our feelings show – these may not be shared, leading to miscommunication.

- ◆ **Assuming the audience is interested** when they are not makes a talk very difficult to deliver.

- ◆ **Assuming the receiver has the knowledge/capacity** to understand the message creates barriers when their knowledge is low.

- ◆ **Perceived status:** those who perceive themselves to be of a lower status may find it difficult to communicate openly with those they perceive to be of a higher status.

- ◆ **Values and beliefs** become explicit barriers in extreme situations, as in a discussion between an anti-nuclear activist and staff of a nuclear power station. In more ordinary situations the differences are less obvious; for example, one person might give priority to a favoured customer while another believes all customers should be treated equally – this difference might never become explicit in a conversation about customer care.

- ◆ **Lack of trust:** if we do not feel we can trust the other person we tend to conceal our own attitude, setting up barriers.

- ◆ **Personality clash:** the perception that you cannot get on with someone immediately sets up a barrier to communicating with them.

Barker (2000) says that 'Communication is the process of creating shared understanding...displaying the shape of your thinking'. Making your own perceptions clear and recognising those of others will help to achieve shared understanding.

### The organisation

The organisation itself may be a barrier to communication. This may be because of:

- ◆ lack of appropriate channels; for example, you know someone in the organisation has the information you need, but do not know who they are

- a culture which discourages informal communication by insisting on putting everything in writing

- a culture of individualism, so it is difficult to obtain a corporate view

- a culture of conflict leading to withholding or distorting information.

## Overcoming barriers

Referring to 11 types of barrier, Handy (1993) suggests that it is perhaps worth admiring the fact that any sensible communication takes place at all.

It is up to us as sender or receiver to make conditions as satisfactory as possible so that barriers are minimised. Key points are as follows:

- Have a clear purpose

- Select the right medium, and use it in an appropriate way

- Anticipate noise and differences between yourself and others.

Handy (1993) suggests that as well as removing causes of blockage we should:

- use more than one communication net

- encourage two-way rather than one-way communication

- keep the number of linkages in the communication to as few as possible.

### Activity 3
### Identify barriers in verbal communication

#### Objective

Use this activity to identify barriers in some of your recent communications.

#### Task

1 Identify a recent verbal communication you were involved in, perhaps one that you felt uncomfortable about, and write it down in the space provided (we have given an example).

| Communication I was involved in | Type |
|---|---|
| Giving feedback to Joan on her talk | One to one, in corridor |

2  Reflect on the communication to identify the barriers that may have distorted communication.

3  Note down the barriers under the appropriate headings in the grid below (see the example).

4  Then note how you might have overcome each barrier (solution).

| Type of barrier | Sender | Transmission | Receiver |
|---|---|---|---|
| Environment Barrier | I felt uncomfortable, and assumed Joan would not be receptive | Distractions from passers-by | Joan was surprised at me bringing up the topic |
| Solution | Accept I have a right to give feedback, and avoid assuming how the person will respond | Use a meeting room for privacy | Allow Joan to prepare by making an appointment with her to review her talk |

| Type of barrier | Sender | Transmission | Receiver |
|---|---|---|---|
| Environment Barrier | | | |
| Solution | | | |
| Language Barrier | | | |
| Solution | | | |
| Culture Barrier | | | |
| Solution | | | |

| Type of barrier | Sender | Transmission | Receiver |
|---|---|---|---|
| *Perceptions* Barrier | | | |
| Solution | | | |
| *The organisation* Barrier | | | |
| Solution | | | |
| *Others* Barrier | | | |
| Solution | | | |

## Feedback

You may have been surprised by the number of barriers that crept into your communication. This is not at all unusual.

It is relatively straightforward to eliminate environmental barriers by choosing the appropriate time and place for the communication.

Eliminating 'sender' barriers means thinking though the message in your own mind first. It also means communicating assertively – something you will look at later in this book – and making sure you choose the appropriate medium.

Minimising 'receiver' barriers from your end involves getting to know the receiver – their attitudes and beliefs – so you can see things from their point of view.

## Skills for verbal communications

Conversations form the basis of most verbal communications, including informal discussions, meetings and the various types of interview. William O'Brien (quoted in Senge et al., 1994) suggests that improved conversation is one of four attributes required by winning companies of the twenty-first century, while Senge et al. say that 'most of what passes for conversation in contemporary society is more like a ping-pong game than true talking and thinking together'.

> **Talking and listening must be balanced to gain shared understanding.**

This need for 'deeper' conversations is met by Guirdham's and Barker's definitions of communication.

> Communication means getting your message across so that it is understood, believed and accepted...and also being receptive to what others are saying to you.
>
> Source: *Guirdham* (1995)

> Communication is the process of creating shared understanding...or...displaying the shape of your thinking.
>
> Source: *Barker* (2000)

Barker (2000) describes conversations as 'verbal dances', with the key dynamics of talking and listening, which Senge et al. (1994) call advocacy and inquiry. Talking allows you to put over your point of view, while listening ensures you understand the other person's point of view. Talking and listening must be balanced to gain shared understanding.

## Essential skills

### Listening

Covey's fifth habit (from *The Seven Habits of Highly Effective People*, 1992), 'Seek first to understand, then be understood', underlines the need to listen in order to understand where the other person is coming from and their views and opinions.

Listening involves far more than sitting back and hearing the other person's words. It involves showing the other person you are listening, seeking to understand what they say, and periodically checking out your understanding by reflecting it back to them.

> Listening is about letting the other person speak first and truly
> hearing what is being said without having your own agenda.

Source: *The Herald* (2001)

Active listening is hard work because, unlike talking, it is something
most of us have not been trained to do.

**How to listen**

- Stop talking, to others and to yourself – learn to still the voice
  within

- Imagine the other person's viewpoint – picture yourself doing
  their work, facing their problems, using their language and
  knowing their values

- Look, act and be interested

- Observe non-verbal behaviour to glean meanings beyond
  what is said to you

- Do not interrupt

- Listen between the lines for what is unsaid or unexplained

- Speak only affirmatively, offer no judgement or criticism
  while listening

- Periodically, reflect back what the person has said to ensure
  you understand.

Real listening helps us to put ourselves in the other person's shoes,
which helps to minimise the barriers of differing perceptions and
create common ground for 'shared understanding', which Barker
(2000) says is the basis of communication.

## Reflecting and summarising

At turning points in the conversation it is helpful to both parties to
summarise what has been said so far. For Barker (2000), reflection is
restating the other person's ideas in your own language, and
involves:

- recognising the point they have made

- appreciating the positions from which they say it

- understanding the beliefs that inform that position.

Summarising goes beyond the periodic reflection involved in active
listening, since it draws together the views of both parties. For
example, in meetings it is helpful if the chairperson periodically
summarises what has been said/agreed/decided so far.

## Questioning

Questioning goes hand in hand with listening to find out more about what the other person thinks.

Barker (2000) says questions should be used to:

◆ find out facts

◆ check your understanding

◆ help the other person improve their understanding

◆ invite the person to examine your own thinking

◆ request action.

Questions should not be used for negative reasons like making someone look foolish, making yourself look clever, or creating an argument. Table 1.1 describes types of question.

Learning to ask the right types of questions at appropriate points in the conversation is a key communication skill.

| Type of question | Description | Example | Uses |
| --- | --- | --- | --- |
| Closed | Can only be answered with 'yes' or 'no' | Do you know what it would cost? | Useful to focus the discussion |
| Open | Cannot be answered by 'yes' or 'no' | How can we get over that challenge? | Helpful to broaden the discussion/get the person talking |
| Leading | Suggests the answer | Is the best solution to cut our capacity for three months? | To influence |
| Controlling | Takes control | Shall we spend 10 minutes looking at options, then move on to solutions? | To take the lead in a conversation/discussion |
| Probing | Goes into more detail than an earlier question | Can you tell me more about this client? | Digs for further information |
| Reflective | Restate the question to the sender | Joe, that's a good question, what do you think is the best option? | To encourage the person to answer the question themselves |
| Redirected | Restate the question to another person | Joe has raised a relevant question – Jean, what do you think is the best option? | In group discussions to draw in a person who is likely to have a helpful response |
| Overhead | Restate the question, addressed to the whole group | Joe has raised a relevant question – I'd like to ask the group what you think is the best option? | In group discussions to invite anyone to respond, possibly to move away from one person dominating the discussion |
| 'What if' questions | Identify what seems like a block in the person's thinking, and formulate a 'what if' question. | What if you weren't limited by a budget? | To liberate the person's thinking |

**Table 1.1** *Types of question*

### Responding

Guirdham (1995) says that the way we respond to statements made by others has a high impact on the success of communications. She quotes the five types of response identified by Carl Rogers:

◆ evaluative            expresses a judgement

◆ interpretative        reads between the lines

◆ supportive            agrees, backs up

◆ probing               asks for more information

◆ understanding         this is what I think you are saying...

The key is to use an appropriate type of response for a specific situation, and to avoid the habit of overusing one or two types of response.

### Feedback

Many conversations involve giving feedback, which may be informal feedback on someone's opinion or work, or within the formal context of a performance appraisal. It is important to remember to give positive feedback, and that negative feedback should always be constructive.

Feedback will only be understood and accepted if you are trusted by the other person, which means building an ongoing relationship with them. Feedback is more likely to be effective if you:

◆ describe the behaviour rather than the person

◆ describe the behaviour rather than judging it

◆ focus more on positives than negatives

◆ give specific examples

◆ listen to their point of view

◆ own your feedback (I think...I felt...)

◆ check that it has been understood

◆ look for alternative ways forward.

Source: *Guirdham* (1995) and *Knasel et al.* (2000)

## Understanding body language

Verbal communications, be they one to one or in a group, are always accompanied by body language, which comprises a huge range of unconscious physical movements (Heller, 1998). You can use body language to strengthen your message or unwittingly allow it to diminish or even contradict what you say. Similarly, you can read other people's body language to see whether or not it confirms their verbal message.

A few minutes watching a TV interviewer or a comedian will show you the ways in which body language cannot be hidden but at times can be consciously used to emphasise a point.

The following list of 'cues' are sourced from Guirdham (1995), but she warns that they must be carefully interpreted.

◆ **Speech**
The rate, volume and pitch reveal emotions; for example, anger and excitement lead to faster, louder and higher pitched talking.

◆ **Eye contact**
Eye contact is usually lower when one person dislikes another, or if the topic is difficult or embarrassing.

◆ **Facial expression**
Smiling, frowning, pursing the lips, etc., reflect emotions and usually match the expression in the eyes. The range of emotions people are allowed to display at work is limited, so those which cannot be expressed in speech may show in the face instead.

◆ **Posture**
The position assumed by the body may be receptive or defensive. When communication goes well the participants may reflect each other's changes in posture; for example, one leaning forward in response to the other.

◆ **Gestures**
Small movements such as finger tapping on the table, fiddling with hair, etc., may reflect feelings such as boredom or lack of confidence.

## Managing conversations

Barker (2000) gives a simple, four-stage model of conversation remembered by the acronym WASP.

◆ Welcome
Agree your objectives ('I've looked at the plan and I've got some suggestions...'), set the scene and establish the relationship.

◆ Acquire
Gather information from each other using as many angles as possible. Listening and questions are the key skills.

◆ Supply
Summarise what you have learned and start to work out what to do with the information. Remind yourselves of the objectives and think of practical options.

◆ Part
Work out what you have agreed and explicitly agree what happens next – the action.

25

When people interrupt a lot, or parallel conversations start, this may signal that the conversation is going too fast. To slow it down, use reflection, summarise the other person's remark before making your own, and use open questions.

When questions dry up, one person dominates the conversation or people are weary because the conversation is going too slowly, you can speed it up by pushing for action; for example, by asking 'What shall we do?', summarising to conclude this part of the conversation or asking for new ideas.

Barker recommends recording conversations in visual form on a pad or flip chart, to show the 'shape of your thinking'. This has the effect of making the communication process visible, but beware of the danger of the group holding an entirely different conversation while someone is writing.

## Activity 4
## Investigate verbal and non-verbal communication

### Objective

Use this activity to investigate verbal and non-verbal communication.

### Task

1 Over the next few days, look out for examples of non-verbal cues in the way people communicate with you. Look for:

   ◆ facial expressions, such as smiles, frowns, puzzled looks

   ◆ eye contact – direct or avoiding

   ◆ posture – relaxed or tense, confident or nervous

   ◆ gestures – of impatience, anxiety, self-confidence

   ◆ other body language, such as fiddling with things, looking at a watch and so on.

2 Select some of these non-verbal cues and note them down in the grid provided. How do you interpret each cue? For example, if someone avoids looking you in the eye, is this because they are nervous or anxious about something?

3 Then decide what impact each cue has on the communication. Does it confirm what the speaker is saying? Does it give you additional information? Does it contradict what the speaker is saying?

| Non-verbal cue | How you interpret this cue | The impact the cue has on communication |
| --- | --- | --- |
| | | |

## Feedback

Being aware of non-verbal cues can help you to improve communication. You can make a more conscious effort to make sure your non-verbal cues reinforce what you say. You can also become more expert at interpreting other people's cues.

At the same time, it helps to be aware that there may be some cultural differences in the interpretation of non-verbal cues. For example, spatial preferences differ from one culture to another – people with an English background tend to prefer to keep some distance between themselves when talking, whereas people in some Mediterranean cultures tend to be more comfortable when closer to the person with whom they are talking. Another example is where not making eye contact in some cultures is seen as a sign of respect for one's superior. In contrast, in Western cultures, this avoidance may be interpreted as being evasive or not wanting to engage in conversation.

## Activity 5
## Review your verbal communication skills

### Objective

This activity will help you to review how you used the skills of verbal communication in a recent conversation at work.

### Task

1 Use the following questions to help you to review your verbal communication skills. Your perception of your own skills may be different from how others see them, so we suggest you make two copies of the questions and do a swap with a colleague whereby you each fill in the questions for yourself and then for the other person.

2 Respond to the questions in the grid by ticking the appropriate box at the end of each question.

| How good are you/is your colleague at: | Very poor | Poor | OK | Good | Very good |
|---|---|---|---|---|---|
| *Listening* | | | | | |
| ◆ giving the other person your full attention? | ☐ | ☐ | ☐ | ☐ | ☐ |
| ◆ seeing things from their point of view? | ☐ | ☐ | ☐ | ☐ | ☐ |
| ◆ listening between the lines? | ☐ | ☐ | ☐ | ☐ | ☐ |
| *Reflecting and summarising* | | | | | |
| ◆ periodically reflecting back in your own words what you have understood in a conversation? | ☐ | ☐ | ☐ | ☐ | ☐ |
| ◆ summarising what has been said/agreed? | ☐ | ☐ | ☐ | ☐ | ☐ |
| ◆ relating the summary to the objective of the conversation/ agenda item? | ☐ | ☐ | ☐ | ☐ | ☐ |
| *Questioning* | | | | | |
| ◆ knowing which type of question to use when you need more information? | ☐ | ☐ | ☐ | ☐ | ☐ |
| ◆ avoiding using leading questions? | ☐ | ☐ | ☐ | ☐ | ☐ |
| ◆ using 'what if?' questions to help unblock the other person's thinking? | ☐ | ☐ | ☐ | ☐ | ☐ |
| *Responding* | | | | | |
| ◆ knowing when a supportive response is needed? | ☐ | ☐ | ☐ | ☐ | ☐ |
| ◆ knowing how to give an interpretive response? | ☐ | ☐ | ☐ | ☐ | ☐ |
| ◆ avoiding giving a habitual type of response? | ☐ | ☐ | ☐ | ☐ | ☐ |

| How good are you/is your colleague at: | Very poor | Poor | OK | Good | Very good |
|---|---|---|---|---|---|
| *Feedback* | | | | | |
| ◆ describing behaviour rather than the person? | ☐ | ☐ | ☐ | ☐ | ☐ |
| ◆ giving specific examples? | ☐ | ☐ | ☐ | ☐ | ☐ |
| ◆ being constructive? | ☐ | ☐ | ☐ | ☐ | ☐ |
| *Reading and using body language* | | | | | |
| ◆ reading the messages that are hidden in posture and gestures? | ☐ | ☐ | ☐ | ☐ | ☐ |
| ◆ identifying when body language conflicts with the verbal message? | ☐ | ☐ | ☐ | ☐ | ☐ |
| ◆ using body language in order to reinforce the message? | ☐ | ☐ | ☐ | ☐ | ☐ |

## Feedback

You probably found that you are good at some skills and not so good at others. Furthermore, you probably found some discrepancies between your perceptions and those of your colleague about your skills. These may have boosted your confidence in some skills, while pointing to areas for improvement in others.

Fill in the following action plan for the skills you most need to develop.

| Areas to improve | Action to take |
|---|---|
| | |

# ◆ Recap

### Explore models of effective interpersonal communication

◆ Communication involves an exchange of meaning, achieved through the processes of coding, transmission, decoding and feedback.

◆ Transactional analysis describes three ego states (behaviour patterns) that each of us can adopt when interacting with others: Parent, Adult and Child. The ideal transaction is Adult to Adult.

### Identify factors influencing organisational communication

◆ Organisational culture has an impact on communication, influencing the extent to which organisations codify and diffuse information.

◆ Organisational trends, including new media, team and project working and delayering, mean that communication is now more direct, informal and immediate.

### Identify the main barriers to effective communication

◆ The main barriers include physical surroundings, language and jargon, and cultural diversity.

◆ Barriers can be overcome by paying attention to the context of communication, selecting the right medium and trying to see things the way the receiver does.

### Skills for improving verbal communication

◆ Listening, reflecting, summarising, questioning, responding and feedback are essential skills for verbal communication.

◆ When your body language or tone of voice is inconsistent with the words you are using, your overall message is diminished and can even be contradicted.

#  More @

**Adair, J. (1997)** *Effective communication: the most important management tool of all*, **Pan**
This book explores basic communication skills and then goes further to look at presentations, visual aids, interviews, appraisals, giving and receiving criticism, and communication between departments

Barker, A. (2000) *Improve Your Communication Skills*, Kogan Page

Isaacs, W. (1999) *Dialogue and the Art of Thinking Together: A Pioneering Approach to Communicating in Business and in Life*, Bantam Doubleday Dell Publishing Group
This book explores the pivotal role of dialogue in successful organisations and the skills that are involved in meaningful conversations.

Murdoch, A. and Scutt, C. (2002) 3rd edition, *Personal Effectiveness*, Butterworth-Heinemann.
This is a core text exploring how to develop the behaviour and skills of effective performance. See the chapters on communication and presentation.

Seely Brown, J. et al. (2004) *Storytelling in Organizations: Why Storytelling Is Transforming 21st Century Organizations and Management*, Butterworth-Heinemann
Learn how story telling can help you become a more relevant, powerful and memorable communicator.

Check out **www.mindtools.com** to develop your understanding of how to communicate effectively – to individuals and groups, via spoken communications, written communications and even electronic communications.

Full references are provided at the end of the book.

# 2 Behaving assertively

Being assertive is not the same as being aggressive. Being assertive means saying what you want and believe, but without attacking or putting others down. It is based on equality between people – despite differences in ability or status – and in the belief that all people (including yourself) should be treated fairly and with respect.

The great thing about genuine assertive behaviour is that it tends to promote the same kind of behaviour in others. It means that your relationship is based on mutual frankness, honesty and fairness.

This sounds like common sense but in reality is quite difficult. We are conditioned by our upbringing and by our experience to behave in certain ways. We might be told to put on a brave face, not to let people mess us around or to respect authority. Some of us, particularly women, have been brought up to put other people's needs before our own. These beliefs are buried deep in our subconscious and can lead us to react in ways that are contrary to what our thinking brain is telling us to do.

In this theme, you will:

- Identify the characteristics of assertive, aggressive and submissive behaviours and review how you behave in particular situations
- Identify the factors that hinder assertiveness and trigger aggressive or submissive behaviour
- Explore techniques for developing assertive behaviour in threatening or difficult situations
- Plan to behave more assertively in a particular situation.

## Understanding assertiveness

Behaviour is commonly categorised into three types: aggressive, submissive and assertive.

**Assertive people learn the skills of compromise and negotiation.**

When behaving aggressively, people want to win at all costs. They think their rights are more important than other people's, and they appear to be very confident by using 'I' a lot, speaking loudly and using threatening body language.

When behaving submissively, people feel unsure of themselves and want to avoid conflict. They tend to mumble, speak softly and use body language to try to make themselves look smaller.

Both aggressive and submissive behaviours stem from low self-esteem. In aggressive behaviour the person takes the 'fight' reaction to feeling threatened, whereas with submissive behaviour the person takes the 'flight' response to threat.

When behaving in an assertive way, the person has high self-esteem and is therefore able to express their needs, wants and opinions in an open and honest way. They speak clearly and reflect their confidence in an open posture. They aim for compromises where both parties 'win'.

Table 2.1 summarises the typical characteristics of the three behaviour types.

| | Aggressive behaviour | Assertive behaviour | Submissive behaviour |
|---|---|---|---|
| Stems from: | Low self-esteem | High self-esteem | Low self-esteem |
| Feelings: | I'm OK, you're not OK | I'm OK, you're OK (*Harris*, 1995) | I'm not OK, you're OK |
| Key words: | You should/ought | I think/feel | Maybe, sorry |
| Voice: | Shouts | Calm voice | Mumbles |
| Body language: | Points, leans forward, stares | Open posture, comfortable eye contact | Closed posture – crossed arms and legs – little eye contact |

**Table 2.1** *Characteristics of behaviour types*

Gillen (1992) suggests that managers who behave in a predominantly:

◆ aggressive way – tend to put people down, ignore their views, be intolerant of mistakes and dictate how staff should behave, all of which invite resentment

◆ submissive way – try to be nice, are easily put upon and place more emphasis on maintaining smooth relationships than achieving results, all of which invite cynicism

◆ assertive way – are clear about their purpose, involve others, are creative, flexible and output oriented.

As always, there are dangers in labelling people. In reality we all adopt different behaviour types at different times and in different situations. For example, one person's friends might be surprised to hear that their apparently assertive social companion behaves in a much more submissive way at work or in a more aggressive way when feeling vulnerable. So, there is no such thing as an 'assertive person'.

In assertive thinking the emphasis is on the behaviour rather than the person. When dealing with someone who has behaved in an aggressive way, it is easier for both parties if you confront their behaviour rather than them as a person.

Behaving assertively is not, as is sometimes imagined:

♦ cold and unfeeling

♦ the same as aggressive behaviour

♦ a guarantee that you will get what you want.

> Being assertive, I believe, springs from a fulcrum of equality. It springs from balance between self and others, from being human, being less restrained by doubt and insecurity so that you can become more fully true to yourself in every way.

Source: *Dickson* (2000)

## A different model of behaviour types

Gillen (1992) agrees that aggressive and submissive behaviours are opposite ends of a spectrum. However, she proposes that assertiveness is not a compromise in between aggresssiveness and submissiveness, but a completely separate option.

Using your responses to the series of questions Gillen poses in *Assertiveness for Managers* (1992), you can plot your 'assertiveness profile' on three axes, as shown in Figure 2.1 for a person with a mainly assertive profile.

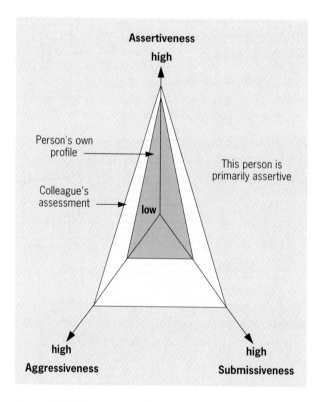

**Figure 2.1** *Plotting assertiveness profile*

Source: *Adapted from Lifeskills Associates Ltd* (1988)

Gillen suggests plotting your own profile, and then asking someone else to complete it for you so you get an idea of how your perception of yourself differs from that of colleagues/friends/family.

# Advantages of assertiveness

Lifeskills Associates Ltd (1988) report that research findings show assertive people to be more confident, less punishing of others, less frustrated, less anxious and more proactive. They explain that proactivity leads to high esteem which in turn improves mental health, and that all these qualities reinforce each other.

In the work context, Back and Back (1999) suggest that behaving more assertively will help you to be more effective in your job because assertion tends to breed assertion. They quote the example of a boss asking a member of his team to take on some more work. The person responds, 'I appreciate you'd like this work done by the end of the month; however, I don't see how I can fit it into my current workload.' This assertive response is likely to lead to a renegotiation of the workload, and to the important additional work being done. Using the transactional analysis approach you looked at earlier, it is an example of Adult-to-Adult communication.

Back and Back give the following general benefits of assertion at work:

♦ increased chance of your needs being met – even when your needs conflict with another person, by being clear and open you can find a solution which is acceptable to you both

♦ greater confidence in yourself – being able to deal with difficult situations makes you feel OK about yourself, even when your needs are not fully met

♦ greater confidence in others – being confident in yourself helps you recognise the strengths of others

♦ increased responsibility for your own behaviour – you move away from blaming others to taking responsibility

♦ taking the initiative is easier as you are not afraid of failure or making a mistake

♦ saving energy – not being preoccupied with upsetting others/losing out saves nervous energy.

## Being assertive does not mean you necessarily get what you want

Lifeskills Associates point out that being an assertive person helps us communicate our needs and feelings, but does not necessarily guarantee we will always get what we want. Assertive people learn the skills of compromise and negotiation. On the other hand, aggressive people use their power and do not concern themselves with the rights of others, so they may be more successful in terms of power or material wealth. However, assertive people sleep better at night because they are more at ease with themselves.

**Relating assertiveness to management theories**

Gillen reviews assertiveness in relation to accepted management theory and concludes that:

♦ assertiveness fits with McGregor's Theory Y where people are assumed to be capable of self-direction and responsibility

♦ assertiveness helps people to meet their needs for security, belonging and self-esteem in Maslow's hierarchy of needs

♦ accepting people's individual rights (an essential aspect of assertiveness) acts as a motivator in Herzberg's model for motivation

♦ applying Tannenbaum and Schmidt's situational leadership model, assertive managers start with high task/low people style, then move to the high task/high people style of leadership.

Source: *Derived from Gillen* (1992)

## Choosing not to be assertive

If you can act assertively, you are free to choose whether or not you will. If you are unable to act assertively, you have no choices; you will be governed by others, and your well-being will suffer.

Source: *Alberti and Emmons* (1978)

When you have learned to think in an assertive way and practised the techniques, it does not mean you will always choose to behave assertively.

You might choose not to behave assertively because, for example:

♦ the situation is a tough one and you do not yet have sufficient confidence to tackle it in an assertive way

♦ being assertive is a new behaviour and you need to avoid dramatic change which might damage your relationships

♦ the other party is particularly sensitive and you do not want them to feel hurt

♦ you simply do not have the energy to adopt assertive behaviour at the time.

**Assertiveness as an individual choice**

Assertiveness is concerned with making choices, and therefore it is important that individuals choose for themselves whether they wish to make these changes or not. They need to understand just what is entailed and be reassured that any changes they make will be gradual and supported. We are creatures of habit and familiarity is often the safest route to take. Relationships are complex to say the least, and when one partner begins to assert themselves the other is likely to feel threatened and may resist change.

Source: *Holland and Ward* (1990)

## Activity 6
### Explore how you behave in a range of situations

### Objective

Use this activity to explore the types of behaviour you use in a range of situations.

### Task

1 Use the following table to identify the range of behaviour types that you use. You will probably find that you use a wide range. Think about situations that you find threatening to identify aggressive behaviour (the fight response) and submissive behaviour (the flight response).

2 Write at least six situations in the appropriate places in the table (see the example).

3 Below each situation, briefly describe the key characteristics of your behaviour. Use Table 2.1 to help you to classify your behaviour.

| | Aggressive behaviour | Assertive behaviour | Submissive behaviour |
|---|---|---|---|
| *Situations at work* | | | |
| Situation | When Paul annoys me by refusing to make a decision | | |
| My behaviour | I feel angry, raise my voice, and start to lecture him that we're short of time | | |

| | Aggressive behaviour | Assertive behaviour | Submissive behaviour |
|---|---|---|---|
| *Situations at work*<br>Situation | | | |
| My behaviour | | | |

| | Aggressive behaviour | Assertive behaviour | Submissive behaviour |
|---|---|---|---|
| *Situations at work*<br>Situation | | | |
| My behaviour | | | |

| | Aggressive behaviour | Assertive behaviour | Submissive behaviour |
|---|---|---|---|
| *Situations at work*<br>Situation | | | |
| My behaviour | | | |

| | Aggressive behaviour | Assertive behaviour | Submissive behaviour |
|---|---|---|---|
| *Other situations*<br>Situation | | | |
| My behaviour | | | |

| | Aggressive behaviour | Assertive behaviour | Submissive behaviour |
|---|---|---|---|
| *Other situations*<br>Situation | | | |
| My behaviour | | | |

| | Aggressive behaviour | Assertive behaviour | Submissive behaviour |
|---|---|---|---|
| *Other situations*<br>Situation | | | |
| My behaviour | | | |

## Feedback

While one behaviour type may predominate, you should have identified situations where you behave in different ways. If you found this difficult, you could ask a colleague or friend to help you because they are likely to see you in a different way.

Recognising situations where you behave in aggressive or submissive ways is the first step to changing your response in these situations to an assertive one.

# Getting to assertive thinking

Looking broadly at being assertive at work, Back and Back (1999) identify a range of reasons why people come to be non-assertive:

◆ not accepting your assertive rights; for example, if you do not accept that you have the right to be clear about what is expected of you, you will not ask for clarification about a job you are unsure of

◆ negative self-talk; for example, the thought 'I'll never be as good as Pete at getting my ideas across' leads you to put your ideas forward very tentatively

◆ fear of unpleasant consequences of assertion; for example, a colleague may be angry if you say 'no' to a request

◆ perceiving situations or people as threatening; for example, a lack of confidence may lead to you saying little in meetings.

Further blocks come from confusing assertion and aggression, equating non-assertion with politeness and confusing non-assertion with helpfulness.

## Rights

If your manager asked you to work during one of your holiday weeks, you would probably feel that your right to annual leave as specified in your contract of employment was being infringed. Equally important, but less visible, are the unwritten rights associated with assertive behaviour.

### General rights

General rights range from the Universal Declaration of Human Rights through the laws of the land to the rights of the individual. As an individual, I have the right:

- to make mistakes
- to set my own priorities
- for my needs to be considered just as important as the needs of other people
- to refuse requests without feeling guilty
- to express myself, so long as I do not violate the rights of others
- to judge my own behaviour, thoughts and emotions, and to take responsibility for the consequences.

Source: *Adapted from Langrith, quoted in Guirdham* (1995)

Standing up for your rights while respecting the rights of the other person is the basis for the 'I win/You win' approach to assertive behaviour.

## Job rights

Focusing on the work context, Back and Back (1999) give the following rights which many people feel they have in their jobs:

- to be clear what is expected of me
- to know how my manager sees my performance
- to do my job in my own way once objectives and constraints are agreed
- to make mistakes from time to time
- to have a say in choosing people who work for me
- to expect work of a certain standard from my staff
- to criticise the performance of staff when it falls below standard
- to be consulted about decisions that affect me
- to take decisions that affect my department or area of work
- to refuse unreasonable requests while respecting the rights of the other person.

Source: *Back and Back* (1999)

When reading through these lists of rights, you may have felt there were some you agreed with, while you were not so sure about others. The rights you are not sure about could well be associated with non-assertive behaviour. Back and Back (1999) point out that it is one thing to understand rights and agree with them, but quite another to accept and act on them. They suggest that the following questions might help.

## Questions for exploring rights

Ask:

- Do I easily give up this right?
- How often do I have to remind myself of this right?
- Why do I have difficulty accepting this right?

◆ How does not accepting this right affect my work/social life/relations with others?

Say, I do have the right to...

## Rights in difficult situations

Gillen (1992) lists the rights people have in a range of difficult situations. Table 2.2 is an example of rights when being reprimanded or criticised.

| Your rights | Their rights |
|---|---|
| Respect, dignity | Agreed standards of performance |
| Fair treatment | Attempt to change others' behaviour where it affects them |
| Not to feel threatened | Constructively criticise |
| Make reasonable mistakes | Be listened to |
| Bring criticism into the open | Honesty |
| Defend self from unjust criticism | |
| Be listened to | |
| Good working relationships | |

**Table 2.2** *Exploration of rights*          Source: *Gillen* (1992)

## Responsibilities

As already mentioned, assertiveness rights are balanced with the general responsibility of respecting the rights of the person you are dealing with. Further, each right has its own attached responsibilities. For example, Back and Back (1999) quote the responsibilities associated with the right to do your job in your own way once objectives and constraints are agreed: to abide by the constraints and to use your time productively in working towards the objectives.

# Activity 7
## Review your rights

### Objective

This activity will help you to review those rights you agree with and those you are not comfortable with.

One reason for not behaving in an assertive way is that we may deny our rights or those of other people, for example, if we do not feel it is acceptable to make mistakes, we are likely to get angry with ourselves or others when mistakes inevitably occur. Reviewing our stance on rights, even if we choose to reject some of them, clarifies where we stand.

### Task

1　Review the lists of rights in the following table.

2　For each right, decide whether or not you understand it, agree with it, accept it. It is quite possible to mentally agree with a right, but not accept it.

3　If you have difficulty deciding, ask yourself the following questions:

◆　Do I easily give up this right?

◆　How often do I have to remind myself of this right?

◆　Why do I have difficulty accepting this right?

◆　How does not accepting this right affect my work/social life/relations with others?

| I have the right: | Understand Yes　No | Agree Yes　No | Accept Yes　No |
|---|---|---|---|
| *General rights* | | | |
| ◆ to make mistakes | ☐　☐ | ☐　☐ | ☐　☐ |
| ◆ to set my own priorities | ☐　☐ | ☐　☐ | ☐　☐ |
| ◆ for my needs to be considered as being as important as the needs of other people | ☐　☐ | ☐　☐ | ☐　☐ |
| ◆ to refuse requests without feeling guilty | ☐　☐ | ☐　☐ | ☐　☐ |
| ◆ to express myself, so long as I do not violate the rights of others | ☐　☐ | ☐　☐ | ☐　☐ |
| ◆ to judge my own behaviour, thoughts and emotions, and to take responsibility for the consequences | ☐　☐ | ☐　☐ | ☐　☐ |

| I have the right: | Understand | | Agree | | Accept | |
|---|---|---|---|---|---|---|
| | Yes | No | Yes | No | Yes | No |
| *Rights at work* | | | | | | |
| ◆ to be clear about what is expected of me | ☐ | ☐ | ☐ | ☐ | ☐ | ☐ |
| ◆ to know how my manager sees my performance | ☐ | ☐ | ☐ | ☐ | ☐ | ☐ |
| ◆ to do my job in my own way once objectives and constraints are agreed | ☐ | ☐ | ☐ | ☐ | ☐ | ☐ |
| ◆ to make mistakes from time to time | ☐ | ☐ | ☐ | ☐ | ☐ | ☐ |
| ◆ to have a say in choosing people who work for me | ☐ | ☐ | ☐ | ☐ | ☐ | ☐ |
| ◆ to expect work of a certain standard from my staff | ☐ | ☐ | ☐ | ☐ | ☐ | ☐ |
| ◆ to criticise the performance of staff when it falls below standard | ☐ | ☐ | ☐ | ☐ | ☐ | ☐ |
| ◆ to be consulted about decisions that affect me | ☐ | ☐ | ☐ | ☐ | ☐ | ☐ |
| ◆ to take decisions that affect my department or area of work | ☐ | ☐ | ☐ | ☐ | ☐ | ☐ |
| ◆ to refuse unreasonable requests | ☐ | ☐ | ☐ | ☐ | ☐ | ☐ |
| Other people have the same rights | ☐ | ☐ | ☐ | ☐ | ☐ | ☐ |

Source: *Back and Back* (1999)

## Feedback

> You are likely to find it easiest to act assertively when those rights that you fully accept are involved. For situations involving those rights that you do not accept, it will probably be difficult to act in an assertive way. You may want to discuss these rights further with a colleague or friend.

## Review your self-talk

Another approach to assertive thinking is to review the self-talk which goes on in our heads, sometimes known as 'inner dialogue'.

For example, 'I'll be the person with least influence at this meeting, so there's not much point in saying anything' is negative self-talk in which the person denies their right to express their opinions, and is likely to result in submissive behaviour. More positive self-talk could be, 'I may be the most junior person at the meeting, but I have a responsibility to give my views. I'll express my views clearly and concisely. Even if I have no influence on the decision, I will have done as much as I can.' From this starting point the person is far more likely to feel good about himself or herself and contribute in an assertive way.

**Positive self-talk leads to positive expectations.**

Positive self-talk leads to positive expectations of a situation and to positive behaviour. It does not guarantee the required outcome will be achieved, but it does increase the chances.

> When problems arise, we frequently behave by default rather than by design. Default behaviour is usually an adult version of our fight or flight instinct and the associated behaviours we learned as a child. The behaviours are the result of a search through our mental data bank to see what sort of situation it is and how we normally behave in it.

Source: *Gillen* (1992)

The way we respond to a situation, including our self-talk, depends on our previous experiences and our attitudes. Alberti and Emmons (1978) suggest that interpersonal fears are a key source of unassertive behaviour, including fears of criticism, rejection, anger, aggression, hurting others, and people in authority. They contend that, just as these fears were learned, they can also be unlearned, using relaxation to desensitise yourself to the fear.

Back and Back (1999) give the following steps for developing positive self-talk for a situation:

◆ Identify the situation you will soon face

◆ Listen to your self-talk – avoid judging it at this stage – cover your anticipated behaviour, their anticipated behaviour and the consequences for you

◆ Challenge your self-talk to identify flaws; for example, generalisations, denial of rights, assumptions, illogical thought

◆ Replace faulty elements with positive self-talk – cover your rights, their rights and your anticipated behaviour

◆ Practise the positive self-talk to yourself.

Table 2.3 gives examples of converting negative self-talk to positive self-talk.

| Negative self-talk | Flaw | Positive self-talk |
|---|---|---|
| It was disastrous that Ann made that mistake | Exaggeration. Denial of Ann's right to make mistakes | Ann's mistake created real problems but was not disastrous. I can point them out. I can keep my cool. I can get her to change |
| If I ask a question when I don't understand, I'll slow the meeting down and they may think I'm thick | Denies my right to say I don't understand | I can't contribute effectively if I don't understand. So I have the right to ask for clarification. It doesn't mean I'm thick |

**Table 2.3** *Examples of conversion to positive self-talk*

**Ways to build confidence**

♦ Talk positively to yourself

♦ Acknowledge your strengths

♦ Celebrate behaviour you like

♦ Treat yourself

♦ Look after your health

♦ Take time and space for yourself

♦ Seek help and support when you need it

♦ Get to know yourself.

Source: *Holland and Ward* (1990)

# Activity 8
## Write positive self-talk

## Objective

Use this activity to convert faulty self-talk to positive self-talk as the basis for assertive behaviour.

## Task

1 Select three situations for which you would like your behaviour to be more assertive, and for which your self-talk is negative. Use a mix of situations from the past and situations you know you will have to face shortly, and note each one in the table provided.

2 Reflect on each situation, imagining yourself when it arose, and identify the self-talk that went on/is going on inside your head.

3 Write the self-talk in the second column of the table.

4 Reflect on the situation again to identify the habits, beliefs or attitudes that led to the negative self-talk. Identify the flaw in the self-talk, for example, exaggeration, denial of a right, assumption, inappropriate belief etc., and note it in the table.

5 Write some more appropriate, positive self-talk (see the example in the table.)

| Situation | Negative self-talk | Flaw | Positive self-talk |
| --- | --- | --- | --- |
| Being asked to give a talk to a large group | I can't possibly do this. I've never been able to get up in front of people. I'll have to make an excuse | Exaggeration Denying myself the right to develop skills | Talking to a group is a challenge for me. I'd like to develop this skill. I need to do it in stages, so I'll ask my boss if I can do a presentation to the team first |

## Feedback

It takes time to change ingrained ways of thinking and responding, so you will need to be alert to your self-talk. Start off with some relatively minor situations to build your confidence in challenging your self-talk. Find ways to repeat your new self-talk to yourself as often as possible so that it eventually replaces your old response.

## Techniques for behaving assertively

There are a number of techniques which you can use alongside assertive thinking to contribute to assertive behaviour.

Back and Back (1999) summarise assertiveness as:

◆ standing up for your own rights in such a way that you do not violate the other person's rights

◆ expressing your needs, wants, opinions, feelings and beliefs in direct, honest and appropriate ways.

Guirdham describes basic assertion as:

> Stating clearly, concisely and usually without justification, what you want, what you think or how you feel.

Source: *Guirdham* (1995)

Examples of assertive statements include:

◆ 'Excuse me, I'd like to finish what I'm saying.'

◆ 'I need to be away by five o'clock.'

◆ 'I feel very pleased with the way the issue has been resolved.'

Each of these statements is clear, specific, direct, honest and uses 'I' statements.

As well as the content of the message, we need to consider the way it is delivered. Messages are reinforced by using appropriate body language, for example an open posture and good eye contact. They are further reinforced by speaking calmly, slowly and with an even voice. Basic assertion is often used at the start of a conversation or where your views are being ignored. It can also be used to give praise, compliments or information to other people. For a more complex situation you could prepare basic assertions to complete the following phrases:

◆ 'Max, I'd like to talk to you about...'

◆ 'As I see it...'

◆ 'So what I'd like to happen is...'

Basic assertion on its own can be very helpful, but for many situations it needs to be refined with more techniques or it can sound abrupt and inconsiderate of the other person.

## Techniques

Guirdham (1995) claims that assertive behaviour is natural behaviour – what we all do in situations that do not seem difficult or threatening. The trick is to extend that behaviour to situations that do worry us. Table 2.4 summarises a range of tools for assertive behaviour.

| Technique | Description | When to use | Example |
|---|---|---|---|
| Self-disclosure | Sharing your thoughts/ feelings | To show trust and openness, and to show that emotions and feelings are legitimate areas for discussion | *I feel a little apprehensive about this discussion...* |
| Responsive | Question to find out where the other person stands | To find out their position; for example, to help find a workable compromise | *What problems does that create for you?* |
| Empathy | Letting the person know you appreciate their position | To show you appreciate their side of things | *I appreciate you want to say something, and I will listen. I'd like to finish what I'm saying first* |
| Broken record | Repeating your main point until you get a response. Keep the message direct and concise | When your point (for example, a request) is being ignored | *Excuse me, I'd like to finish what I'm saying* |
| Fogging | Reflect back what the other person said to you. Avoid being emotional or using judgement | When you are being criticised or put down. Fogging protects your self-esteem | You look terrible this morning. Those clothes look as though they have never seen a washing machine and your hair... *You are probably right, I don't look my best this morning* |
| Negative enquiry | Question to find out more about a negative thing the other person has said about you | To actively prompt criticism, and find out whether the criticism is genuine or a put-down | You'll find that difficult because you're so shy *In what ways do you think I'm too shy?* |
| Discrepancy | A statement to point out the differences between what was agreed and what is about to happen | When the situation is not as you expected, and you need clarification | *As I understood it we agreed that project A was priority. Now you're asking me to give more time to project B. I'd like to clarify which is now priority* |
| Consequence | Statement to inform the person of the consequence of not changing their behaviour | As a last resort to point out consequences | *I'm not prepared, Paul, to let any of my staff co-operate with yours on the project unless you give them access to the same facilities* |

**Table 2.4** *Assertiveness techniques*

Source: *Derived from Back and Back* (1999), *Gillen* (1992), *Guirdham* (1995) *and Lindenfield* (1986)

All the examples of assertive statements in Table 2.4 need to be delivered in an assertive way. The assertive statement, 'Excuse me, I'd like to finish what I'm saying', delivered in a loud voice, could easily backfire if the receiver interprets it as an aggressive message.

In practice, assertive behaviour involves using a combination of tools to suit the needs of both the situation at the outset and the conversation as it progresses.

## Tackling difficult situations

The following list shows a range of the situations which some people find threatening – of course, you will find that some of them pose no threat, while others make you uneasy:

- dealing with anger in others
- dealing with put-downs
- aggression/passive behaviour in others
- giving and receiving criticism
- giving and receiving praise
- resolving conflict
- negotiations
- making and dealing with complaints
- making and refusing requests
- delegating unpleasant tasks
- talking to a poor listener
- handling persistent salespeople
- telling your team about tough targets
- meetings.

The model illustrated in Figure 2.2 shows one way of preparing to deal with difficult situations.

In Figure 2.3 this model is applied to the situation of handling work overload from your boss.

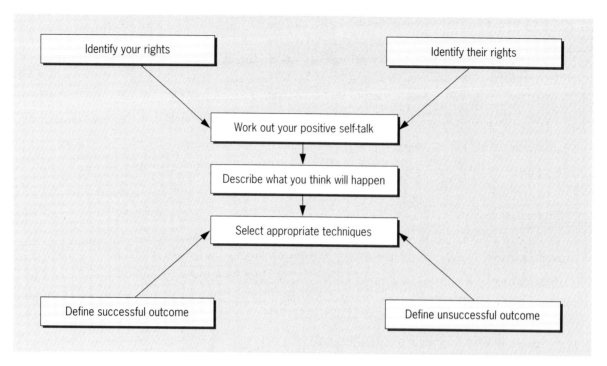

**Figure 2.2** *Model for preparing to deal with difficult situations*

Source: *Adapted from Gillen* (1992)

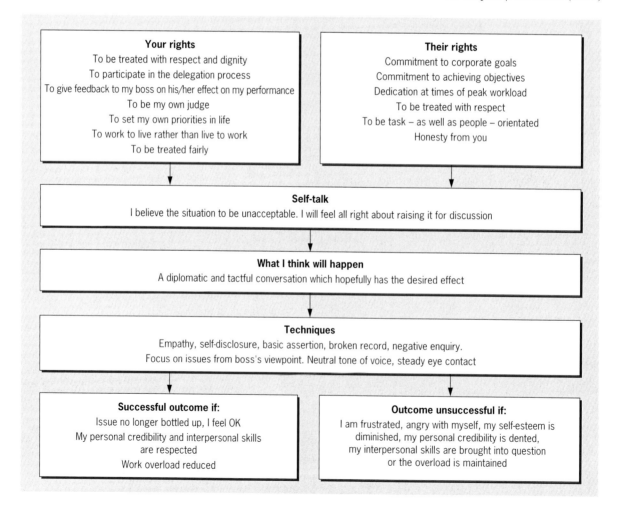

**Figure 2.3** *Preparing to handle work overload in an assertive way*

Source: *Adapted from Gillen* (1992)

# In practice

Learning to behave in an assertive way takes both preparation and practice, and is best learned in a group situation where there are opportunities to role-play situations in a safe environment.

Here are some check-points for putting assertiveness into practice:

◆ Start with:

– minor situations where the results do not matter too much

– situations for which you can prepare in advance – on-the-spot assertiveness will come later

– situations where you have a good chance of maintaining your assertion and achieving a mutually acceptable outcome

◆ Prepare thoroughly: your rights and their rights, positive self-talk, the actual words, the delivery, the outcome you hope to achieve

◆ Practise, preferably with a partner

◆ Review what you have learned afterwards

◆ Introduce assertive behaviour gradually – a sudden change can be threatening to relationships at home and at work.

## Activity 9
### Plan to behave assertively in a difficult situation

### Objective

This activity will help you to plan to behave assertively in a difficult situation.

### Task

1 Identify a difficult situation that you need to face. It might be one of the situations you have already considered in Activity 8.

2 Use:

◆ the table of assertiveness techniques (Table 2.4)

◆ the example for preparing to handle work below (Figure 2.3)

◆ the proforma overleaf to help you to prepare to behave in an assertive way.

## Preparing to behave in an assertive way

**Your rights**

**Their rights**

▼ ▼

**Self-talk**

▼

**What I think will happen**

▼

**Techniques**

▼ ▼

**Successful outcome if:**

**Outcome unsuccessful if:**

## Feedback

Thorough preparation, such as you have carried out in this activity, helps to identify any weaknesses in your approach to dealing assertively with a particular situation. Once you have used the method a few times, or adapted it to suit your needs, you will be able to work through the preparation fairly quickly.

Remember to start off by using assertive behaviour in situations that are not too threatening, and where you can accept the outcome if you end up being partially assertive.

# ◆ Recap

### Identify the characteristics of assertive, aggressive and submissive behaviour

◆ Behaving assertively means expressing your needs, opinions and feelings honestly and directly, without violating the other person's rights. It stems from high self-esteem.

◆ It is different from aggressive behaviour where one person seeks to satisfy personal needs at the expense of those of other people, and from submissive behaviour where the needs of other people are allowed to predominate.

### Identify the factors that hinder assertiveness and trigger aggressive or submissive behaviour

◆ Our behaviour is driven by beliefs about how we should react to certain situations and people. These beliefs, developed from our upbringing and experience, are deeply ingrained in our subconscious mind.

◆ When faced with situations that we think will be difficult or threatening, our subconscious beliefs trigger the body's natural fight or flight instincts, leading us to react aggressively or submissively.

### Explore techniques for developing assertive behaviour in threatening or difficult situations.

◆ The first step in becoming more assertive is to check that your expectations of a situation are not negative. Rephrasing negative self-talk so that it is positive helps to promote a positive mindset and the confidence to behave assertively.

◆ Some general guidelines for behaving assertively are to adopt appropriate body language and voice tone, and to use techniques like self-disclosure, empathy, broken record, fogging, negative enquiry, discrepancy and consequence.

### Plan to behave more assertively in a particular situation

◆ Improvement in behaving assertively comes with practice. Start by identifying a range of situations where your current response is either submissive or aggressive.

◆ Prepare to take a more assertive approach by identifying your own rights, developing positive self-talk, planning the assertiveness techniques you will use and the outcome you hope to achieve without violating the rights of the other person.

## More @

**Back, K. and Back, K. (1999)** *Assertiveness at Work,* **Mcgraw-Hill Education**
This is a highly practical text for developing assertiveness in a wide range of situations, including managing upwards, negotiations and during change.

**Gillen, T. (2000)** *Assertiveness,* **CIPD**

**Goleman, D. (2000)** *Working With Emotional Intelligence,* **Bantam**
Progress your work on communication and assertiveness by exploring emotional intelligence: how people manage feelings, interact and communicate. See also **www.eiconsortium.org/ index.html**

**Covey, S. (1992)** *The Seven Habits of Highly Successful People,* **Simon & Schuster**
This is a hugely popular text for developing your personal and professional effectiveness.

Full references are provided at the end of the book.

# 3 Making meetings productive

Properly run meetings save time, increase motivation and productivity, and solve problems. They create new ideas and initiatives, achieve buy-in and diffuse conflict in a way that e-mail simply cannot.

So why do managers complain about meetings? Perhaps because so many meetings are either unnecessary or are badly run. Badly run meetings waste time, money, resources, and are worse than having no meetings at all.

As managers spend around 60 per cent of their time in meetings, it is well worth making sure the time is used productively. This theme looks at how you can get the most out of meetings – first as a participant and second as the person running the meeting.

> **Lack of a clear purpose is a key reason why meetings fail.**

In this theme, you will:

◆ Identify the purpose of meetings and explore why meetings sometimes fail

◆ Review how to prepare for a meeting

◆ Evaluate your skills as a meeting participant

◆ Consider the role of the chairperson and the skills required to chair a meeting.

## Preparing for meetings

Managers are involved in a range of different types of meeting, including:

◆ impromptu meetings to resolve an immediate problem

◆ small informal meetings (for example, regular team meetings, project meetings, client meetings)

> **If you fail to prepare then prepare to fail.**

◆ large formal meetings with set procedures (for example, board meetings, committees).

Most meetings are still held face to face, but teleconferencing, video conferencing and computer links are increasingly being used to save the time and cost of people having to meet at one location.

**Using technology**
E-mail is suitable for information dissemination and consultations. The 'meeting' can extend over days or weeks as members participate in a 'virtual' conference site, commenting on an issue or problem. Microsoft Outlook® software allows participants to vote on points in a message using 'voting

buttons'. The disadvantage is the accumulation of unnecessary information.

Microsoft® Net Meeting allows for a full-scale meeting in real time using messages typed to a chat board or an audio link (only two people can talk at a time). Ideas can be shown on a whiteboard.

Video conferencing is the most sophisticated form of 'remote meeting'. Participants can all see and hear each other while based at remotely located computers. The hardware required is a camera, video capture card, conferencing software for each participant and a fast Internet connection. The meeting can be videoed and subsequently made available to anyone who was unable to participate.

Source: *Caunt* (2000) *and Hindle* (1998)

## Purpose of the meeting

The starting point in preparing for any meeting is to define its purpose. Caunt (2000) identifies that the main purposes of meetings are to:

◆ impart information

◆ elicit views

◆ stimulate new ideas

◆ motivate a team

◆ reach decisions.

Lack of a clear purpose is a key reason why meetings fail. If people are unclear of the purpose, they are unlikely to prepare adequately and will form their own views of what is to be achieved at the meeting. This results in wasted time and energy, whereas if the purpose is clear, participants can focus on achieving it.

**Why meetings fail**
Barker (1997) reinforces the need for preparation by identifying seven main reasons why meetings fail, of which all except one relate to preparation:

◆ the meeting is unnecessary

◆ the meeting is held for the wrong reason

◆ the objective is unclear

◆ the wrong people are there

◆ poor environment

◆ poor timing

◆ lack of control.

# Is a meeting needed?

Once the purpose is defined the next step is to consider whether a meeting is in fact needed. Meetings are costly in terms of salaries, travel, administration and lost opportunity costs. Barker (1997) suggests meetings are probably the most expensive method of communication, with costs unlikely to be less than several hundred pounds an hour.

Before calling a meeting, check out the alternatives, which include:

◆ an informal meeting with one or two key people

◆ letter, phone, fax, e-mail

◆ conference call.

We often get into the habit of holding regular meetings, so it is worth asking 'What would happen if the meeting were not held?' Sometimes we use meetings as an excuse to avoid other tasks which are difficult to tackle.

The costs of a meeting need to be balanced against the potential benefits, which include:

◆ communicating to a group

◆ meeting face to face

◆ improving the quality of decisions

◆ getting to know people

◆ drawing from a variety of experiences

◆ building the team.

Source: *Fleming* (1997)

On the other hand, Caunt (2000) suggests that there are better ways of imparting information than meetings: people are more creative when working individually; one to one reinforcement and coaching can often achieve more than a motivational team meeting; and meetings have many drawbacks when it comes to decision making.

# Practical preparations

Assuming the purpose of the meeting has been defined, and a meeting is necessary to achieve it, there are a number of practical aspects to preparing for a meeting, which are summarised in Table 3.1. Some aspects are more relevant to large, formal meetings.

While several people may be involved in preparing for the meeting, the chairperson has ultimate responsibility to ensure the preparations are completed.

| Decision/task | Considerations |
|---|---|
| Type of meeting | Impromptu, informal or formal?<br>Regular or one-off?<br>Stand-up meetings keep the time to a minimum<br>Face-to-face meeting or video conference? |
| Who should participate? | Key decision makers<br>Experts or givers of information<br>Opinion formers<br>Others with an interest in the outcomes<br>2–5 people forms cohesive group, but narrower range of skills<br>Over 10 people more difficult to get agreement, but better evaluation of information<br>Some people may only be needed for part of the meeting |
| Time | Consider travel times<br>Allow some notice<br>Fit in with another meeting<br>For an international video conference, check out time differences |
| Location and venue | On-site or off-site? Your office/their office?<br>Where can most people reach easily?<br>Does the venue have suitable facilities?<br>Is it a suitable size?<br>Visit a new venue before booking to check windows, heating, sockets, etc.<br>Check access for any disabled participant |
| Seating | Round table – encourages free discussion<br>Oblong table with chair at head – reinforces hierarchy<br>Seats down each side of table – suggests confrontation<br>Avoid over-comfortable chairs |
| Equipment | Find out what aids are needed and book them (flip chart and pens, overhead projector, PowerPoint hardware, video, etc.)<br>Make sure you know how to use them, or enlist technical support |
| Hospitality | Coffee on arrival?<br>Water on table?<br>Buffet-style lunch encourages mingling |
| Agenda and papers | Send out agenda, background papers and travel directions 1–2 weeks in advance.<br>Liaise with any administrator for the meeting |

**Table 3.1** *Tasks in preparing for a meeting*

Source: *Barker* (1997) *and Hindle* (1998)

## Preparing the agenda

The key document at meetings is the agenda (meaning 'things to be done') which helps people focus on what they have to do – before, during and after the meeting. The more informative the agenda, the more likely it is that people will come well-prepared to make effective contributions. The agenda should include:

◆ title of meeting, date, place and time

◆ apologies for absence

◆ minutes of previous meeting

◆ matters arising from the previous meeting

◆ items to be reported/discussed including:

– required outcome, such as 'decision on', 'share views on'

- name of the person who will talk on the item
- approximate time for the item

◆ any other business

◆ date of next meeting.

For regular meetings the minutes of the last meeting give the start point for preparing the agenda.

For some meetings it is usual to invite agenda items from participants; this process needs to be started well in advance of the meeting. The items should be in a logical order. If one item depends on the decision of another, they should be ordered accordingly.

For impromptu meetings the agenda may be agreed by the participants at the time, either verbally or in writing, perhaps on a flip chart.

## Activity 10
### Make practical preparations for a meeting

### Objective

This activity is the first of a series about preparing and running meetings. Use this activity to prepare for a real meeting.

### Task

1 Use Table 3.1 to plan a forthcoming meeting. This could be a team meeting or a one-off project meeting. It might be a meeting that you will chair or a meeting someone else will chair, but you are responsible for most of the preparations.

2 Write your plan in the blank table overleaf.

## Your preparation plan

| Aspect | Meeting plan |
| --- | --- |
| Type of meeting | |
| Who should participate? | |
| Time | |
| Location and venue | |
| Seating | |
| Equipment | |
| Hospitality | |
| Other aspect | |

## Feedback

After the meeting, review your preparation plan. Consider what went well and what you will do differently next time.

A successful meeting also has a clear purpose and agenda. Activity 11 gives you the opportunity to prepare an agenda for the meeting.

## Activity 11
### Prepare an agenda

## Objective

This activity is one of a series about preparing and running meetings. It will help you to prepare an agenda for a meeting.

You could base your work in this activity on the same meeting you prepared for in Activity 10.

## Task

1  Use the following checklists to prepare your agenda.

   How to prepare the agenda:

   ◆ if appropriate, invite participants to submit items

   ◆ include items arising from minutes of a previous meeting

   ◆ order items in a logical way, taking account of any item, which is dependent on another.

   What to include in the agenda:

   ◆ title of meeting, date, place and time

   ◆ apologies for absence

   ◆ minutes of previous meeting

   ◆ matters arising from the previous meeting

   ◆ items to be reported/discussed including:

     – required outcome, for example, 'decision on', 'share views on'

     – name of the person who will talk on the item

     – approximate time for the item

   ◆ any other business (AOB)

   ◆ date of next meeting.

*Agenda*

### Feedback

The agenda should be circulated with any relevant papers at least a week before the meeting. You could invite comments from participants, for example, ask if there are any other issues that participants feel should be discussed.

After the meeting, review how well your agenda worked in practice.

## Participating in meetings

### Preparing to participate

Preparation before a meeting will help you to feel confident about your position and your contribution, which will in turn make you feel more relaxed and creative during the meeting. There are two main aspects to this preparation: preparing your own information and views, and anticipating the position and views of the other participants (Guirdham, 1995).

**The outcome of a meeting is the joint responsibility of all the participants.**

**General preparation**
The following list summarises preparations which are likely to be necessary before any meeting:

♦ Check the purpose of the meeting

♦ Read the minutes of the previous meeting

♦ Check who will be participating and find out about any participants you do not know

♦ Identify items for which you are required to make an input:
  – your name should be against them on the agenda
  – prepare accordingly (see below)

♦ For other items in which you have an interest:
  – prepare relevant factual information
  – prepare relevant views and opinions
  – anticipate the views/opinions/position of other participants

♦ Consider contacting other participants before the meeting to:
  – exchange information
  – sound out their opinions
  – canvass support.

Source: *Adapted from Hindle* (1998)

The amount of time you spend preparing for a particular meeting will depend on your involvement in the issues and how much you have to contribute. If you feel that your interests are marginal to the meeting, consider whether you should attend for part of the meeting, or not at all, and discuss this with the chairperson.

## Preparing to give a formal contribution

When you are asked to provide specific input to a meeting, thorough preparation is essential. Unless you are absolutely clear what is required, check this out with the chairperson first.

Such inputs could be, for example, a progress report on a project, information on the option of merging two sites, a feasibility report for a new product, views on increasing the product specification, etc. Normally you will have attended previous meetings and be aware of the background to your contribution. However, there may be occasions when you are invited to make a contribution to a meeting you do not normally participate in. This would involve more preparation in terms of finding out about other participants, reading the minutes, etc.

## Steps for preparing a formal contribution

◆ Write down the purpose of your contribution. Include a verb; for example, to inform... justify... influence... propose...

◆ Obtain any background information:

– past information from papers; for example, past minutes, previous reports, the relevant file, other people

– new information from colleagues/experts/journals.

◆ Note the factual information you need to present – how is this best presented? For example, you might use lists, tables, pie charts, diagrams etc.

◆ Note relevant views/opinions – how do you justify them?

◆ Put yourself in other participants' shoes:

– what do they already know about the item?

– what questions/objections/support will they raise?

– how will you respond?

◆ Structure your contribution.

◆ Prepare prompt notes to talk from.

◆ Prepare any visual aids/handouts, etc.

◆ Practise your contribution to keep to the time allowed on the agenda.

You may want to speak informally to other participants before the meeting to find out more about their views, or perhaps to sow the seeds of your ideas in their minds.

**Tips for making a formal contribution**

◆ Prepare any equipment before the meeting

◆ Position yourself so you can be seen by everyone

◆ Wait for the chairperson's cue to start

◆ Say something to gain interest at the outset

◆ Say whether you will take questions at the end (advisable) or as you go along

◆ Use prompt notes, but avoid reading

◆ Consider using overhead projector/PowerPoint slides of key points as prompts to boost your confidence

◆ Make periodic eye contact with all participants

◆ Pick up any non-verbal signs of agreement/confusion/ boredom, etc. and respond accordingly

◆ At the end, summarise your key points

◆ Keep an open mind when listening to questions

◆ Only give out detailed handouts after the presentation or you lose people's attention.

## Skills for participating

Participating constructively in a meeting is essential for a successful outcome and entails using a range of communication skills:

◆ Keeping an open mind – even in negotiations it is important to keep an open mind to another acceptable compromise

◆ Respecting other participants, even when you disagree with them

◆ Listening – linked to an open mind: actively listen to others' contributions, and reflect back what you hear

◆ Using different types of question – open questions to encourage someone to talk, closed questions to focus on specific information, reason, etc.

◆ Putting over your points clearly (see below)

◆ Asking for clarification – if you are not clear, the chances are others also need clarification

◆ Challenging – ask for reinforcement of evidence/viewpoints when you are not convinced, and be prepared for others to ask you

◆ Assisting a weak chair by summarising – if no one else does, summarise key points at the end of an item

◆ Taking accurate notes of decisions, action and other relevant information, and checking your notes with someone else from the meeting.

One way to develop your skills is to watch out for skills being used in meetings you attend, and try out those which you think are effective.

### Using technology

New applications of technology, such as teleconferencing, are playing an increasing role in how communications between groups in organisations are managed. Teleconferencing has been found to be most effective when the participants have met previously and have had an opportunity to socialise.

Here are some tips on how to manage a teleconference meeting:

♦ Allow pauses between speakers, or time is lost while statements are repeated. Teleconferences have their own peculiar rhythm.

♦ Take things slowly – people may be speaking from faraway locations – as with long-distance telephone conversations, there may be a gap before sound gets through

♦ Use your name frequently

♦ Choose your words with care, especially if there is no video link, or there may be misunderstandings

♦ On video, ensure everyone is visible

♦ Do not interrupt other speakers as this can block out the sound from the others.

Source: *Adapted from Caunt* (2000)

## Activity 12
### Evaluate your skill as a meeting participant

### Objective

Use this activity to evaluate your skill as a meeting participant.

### Task

1 Tick one box for each of the statements in the following table.

| | Never | Occasionally | Frequently | Always |
|---|---|---|---|---|
| I allow speakers to finish making their point before I speak | ☐ | ☐ | ☐ | ☐ |
| I am confident when making a point or stating my views | ☐ | ☐ | ☐ | ☐ |
| I am able to concede when I am wrong | ☐ | ☐ | ☐ | ☐ |
| I can control the tone of my voice when I feel nervous | ☐ | ☐ | ☐ | ☐ |
| My body language suggests self-confidence | ☐ | ☐ | ☐ | ☐ |
| I dress appropriately for each meeting I attend | ☐ | ☐ | ☐ | ☐ |
| I listen carefully to what other people are saying in a meeting | ☐ | ☐ | ☐ | ☐ |
| I am thoroughly prepared for each meeting I attend | ☐ | ☐ | ☐ | ☐ |
| I carefully review the minutes of the previous meeting | ☐ | ☐ | ☐ | ☐ |
| I research in advance the views of the other participants | ☐ | ☐ | ☐ | ☐ |
| I know what my objectives are before I attend a meeting | ☐ | ☐ | ☐ | ☐ |
| I share a common purpose with the other participants | ☐ | ☐ | ☐ | ☐ |
| I produce accurate notes of decisions taken, action agreed and other relevant information | ☐ | ☐ | ☐ | ☐ |

Source: *Adapted from Hindle* (1998)

## Feedback

Score your results as follows:

1 – Never                    2 – Occasionally

3 – Frequently               4 – Always

Be as honest as you can: if your answer is 'never', mark 1; if it is 'always', mark 4.

### Score 24 or less
Your skills need all-round attention.

### Score 25–36
You have definite strengths and some areas that need improvement.

### Score 37 or more
You perform well in meetings, but do not become complacent. Continue to prepare well for each meeting you attend.

## Leading meetings

> At least 60% of managers' time is spent in meetings... Meetings can be inspiring, energetic and fun. They can also be dispiriting, demotivating and deadly dull.

Source: Barker (1997)

The course a meeting takes depends on all the participants, and particularly on the person leading it, often designated the 'chairperson'.

## Role of the chairperson

The Open University (1990) identifies two chairing roles:

◆ ensuring the business is completed (traditional chairing role), by:

  – ensuring fair play

  – staying in charge

  – remaining neutral

◆ helping the group carry out its tasks (facilitative role), by:

  – clarifying goals

  – encouraging participation

  – looking for areas of agreement.

The balance of these roles varies for different types of meeting, with the traditional role dominating in more formal meetings. The balance of roles changes within a meeting, with the facilitative role dominating during discussions.

For some regular meetings the roles of chairperson, administrator and minute taker rotate from meeting to meeting.

## Tasks

Table 3.2 summarises the key tasks the chairperson is responsible for during the various stages of the meeting. The chairperson may delegate some of these tasks, but still retains responsibility for them.

A good way to develop chairing skills is to watch how other people tackle the various chairing tasks in the meetings you attend. In your own meetings, try out the techniques you think are particularly effective.

| Task | Comments |
|---|---|
| *Before the meeting* | Prepare agenda, organise venue, etc. |
| Familiarise self with agenda items | Read previous minutes, anticipate difficult items |
| Familiarise self with participants | Identify shy people to be drawn out and dominant people to be kept under control<br>Find out participants' interests and views<br>Anticipate likely conflicts of interest<br>Anticipate likely tactics for a negotiation meeting and prepare your team's tactics |
| *During the meeting* | |
| Opening | Start on time, welcome/introduce participants, state the aims, be positive |
| Pace | Keep to the timings of the agenda items<br>If necessary, delegate a sub-group to continue the item and report back to the next meeting<br>Change position/tone to enliven the pace |
| Facilitate each item | For an item where you have an interest, delegate the chair to another participant<br>Introduce the item, emphasising what is to be discussed, why it is being discussed, the required outcomes and the time available<br>Listen more than you talk so you are alert to understand contributions, keep people focused, clarify points and resolve muddle, judge when a conversation should stop<br>Encourage contributions, drawing out the shy and controlling talkative members<br>Summarise viewpoints/decisions made at the end of each item or within long items<br>Establish who is to take any agreed action |
| Any other business | A well-planned meeting should not generate much 'other business'<br>Decide what is relevant to the meeting, what is irrelevant and what could go on to the next meeting's agenda |
| Close the meeting | Try to end on a positive note<br>Summarise main decisions and actions and check agreement<br>Thank participants<br>Set time, date and place for next meeting |
| After the meeting | Ensure minutes are written up and circulated promptly<br>Monitor progress on action |

**Table 3.2** *Summary of chairperson's tasks*

Source: *Barker (1997), Guirdham (1995) and Hindle (1998)*

## Skills

As well as the general communication skills of listening, using questions and reading body language, Hindle (1998) identifies a series of skills and attitudes which are particularly important for chairing meetings:

◆ firmness in running meetings to time and dealing with problems

◆ ability to summarise points succinctly

◆ flexibility in dealing with different styles of participants

◆ openness and receptiveness in listening to opinions you do not share

◆ fair-mindedness in ensuring all views are aired and given equal consideration.

A further key skill of the chairperson is to balance the various interests of the meeting. For example, in most meetings there is a tension between the time available and achieving the desired outcomes. Sometimes it is appropriate to guide the meeting back to the time constraints, whereas at other times it is more appropriate to gain the agreement of the meeting to extend the time for a particular item. Chairing is an activity which requires thinking on your feet.

Another aspect is to balance the roles of the task, the group and the individual. Adair (1983) argues that in any meeting you need to spend some time on achieving the task, some on attending to the needs of individuals and some on building the team. As team leader, you need to strike a balance between these three things – if, for example, you devote all your energy to driving through the task, then people within the team may feel neglected.

## Dealing with difficult situations

Difficult situations arise in most meetings. Some result from poor planning or chairing; once recognised, they can be remedied for the future. However, many difficulties arise from the personalities involved, and in some cases from deliberately disruptive tactics. Others arise from power games and politics, including the 'hidden agenda' of a participant.

The key is to anticipate difficult situations. Conflicts of interests or personalities can often be anticipated, while difficulties arising in a meeting can be detected by reading negative signs. Signs of anger, withdrawal, boredom or being argumentative are often expressed in body language.

**Tips for dealing with difficult situations**

◆ Anticipate likely difficulties

◆ Repeat the objective of the meeting/item, and challenge people to explain the relevance of their remarks

◆ Avoid being drawn into an argument

◆ Avoid interrupting people

◆ Slow the conversation down – do not mirror the tone, pitch or speed of other people's speech or things escalate

◆ Listen to points being made and display them on a flip chart

◆ Focus on solutions rather than problems

◆ Turn complaints into objectives by asking people to restate them as 'how to' statements

◆ Praise helpful, honest contributions

- ◆ When you need to criticise a comment, criticise the remark, not the speaker
- ◆ Ask for different points of view
- ◆ Stop talk about people not at the meeting.

Source: *Derived from Barker* (1997)

For difficulties that spread into several meetings, it is important to identify the cause. This could be to do with personality; for example, some people like to stir things up, others enjoy an argument. Their views need to be recognised but kept short. Hostility may come from a feeling of powerlessness and may result in anger focused on things that have happened in the past or what 'they' have done. In this case, it is helpful to focus thoughts on the future and move forward.

## Activity 13
### Review how you chaired a meeting

### Objective

Use this activity to review how you chaired a recent meeting.

### Task

1 Think about a meeting you recently chaired, this could be your team meeting or perhaps the meeting you prepared for in Activities 10 and 11.

2 Consider each of the statements in the following chart, and rate your performance in this aspect of chairing meetings.

3 In the 'others' row at the bottom of the chart, add any further aspects of the meeting that come to mind and rate your performance.

| Aspect of chairing the meeting | Very poor | Poor | OK | Good | Very good |
|---|---|---|---|---|---|
| Practical preparation before the meeting (agenda, venue etc.) | ☐ | ☐ | ☐ | ☐ | ☐ |
| Familiarisation with agenda items, minutes and papers | ☐ | ☐ | ☐ | ☐ | ☐ |
| Familiarisation with meeting participants (their characters, interests, views, likely conflicts) | ☐ | ☐ | ☐ | ☐ | ☐ |
| Opening the meeting (start on time, welcome, introductions, state aims, positive start) | ☐ | ☐ | ☐ | ☐ | ☐ |
| Pacing the meeting (keeping to timings) | ☐ | ☐ | ☐ | ☐ | ☐ |
| Balancing the needs of task, group and individual | ☐ | ☐ | ☐ | ☐ | ☐ |

| Aspect of chairing the meeting | Very poor | Poor | OK | Good | Very good |
|---|---|---|---|---|---|
| Thinking on your feet, for example, in deciding whether to overrun the time for an item in the light of new information | ☐ | ☐ | ☐ | ☐ | ☐ |
| Facilitating items (introducing, listening, encouraging contributions, summarising, agreeing action) | ☐ | ☐ | ☐ | ☐ | ☐ |
| Dealing with difficult situations (dominant person, conflict, etc.) | ☐ | ☐ | ☐ | ☐ | ☐ |
| Dealing with AOB (keep to minimum) | ☐ | ☐ | ☐ | ☐ | ☐ |
| Closing the meeting (end positively, summarise decisions and actions, thanks, date of next meeting) | ☐ | ☐ | ☐ | ☐ | ☐ |
| Following up afterwards (writing and circulating minutes, monitoring progress on action) | ☐ | ☐ | ☐ | ☐ | ☐ |
| Others, specify below: | | | | | |
| | ☐ | ☐ | ☐ | ☐ | ☐ |
| | ☐ | ☐ | ☐ | ☐ | ☐ |

## Feedback

Working through this activity should have given you an idea of which chairing skills you need to develop.

# ◆ Recap

**Identify the purpose of meetings and explore why meetings sometimes fail**

◆ Meetings are effective in imparting information, eliciting views and stimulating new ideas, and for team motivation and reaching decisions.

◆ A meeting may fail because of inadequate planning and preparation, low levels of participation by the members or poor chairing. The meeting may also fail if the participants feel that it is unnecessary.

**Review how to prepare for a meeting**

◆ The key tasks in preparing for a meeting include defining its purpose, identifying who needs to attend, selecting a convenient time and location, creating an environment that is conducive to good group communication and distributing an agenda and papers in advance so that participants can prepare.

◆ Prepare to participate in a meeting by familiarising yourself with the meeting purpose, reading papers and previous minutes and preparing for items where you have an interest or need to input, and by anticipating the likely position and views of others.

**Evaluate your skills as a meeting participant**

◆ To participate effectively, you need to keep an open mind, respect and listen actively to the contribution of others, be willing to challenge when you are not convinced and take notes.

◆ There are additional considerations in relation to putting your message across and minimising distractions during virtual meetings, e.g. video or Internet conferences.

**Consider the role of the chairperson and the skills required to chair a meeting**

◆ Chairing a meeting involves two key roles: ensuring the meeting achieves its objectives and getting the best out of the participants.

◆ Effective chairing is achieved by: adopting an authoritative approach; giving succinct summaries; using the skills of listening, questioning and reading body language to encourage contribution from all participants; and being open and fair-minded to ensure all views are aired and given equal consideration.

## ▶▶ More @

Barker, A. (1997) *How to Hold Better Meetings*, Kogan Page

Hindle, T. (1998) *Managing Meetings*, Dorling Kindersley

Barlow, J. et al. (2002) 1st edition, *Smart Videoconferencing: New Habits for Virtual Meetings*, 1st edn, Berrett-Koehler Publishers Inc.,
This book gives practical advice on leading and participating in virtual meetings.

Newstrom, J. and Scannell, E. (1995) *Big Book of Business Games: Icebreakers, Creativity Exercises and Meeting Energizers*, McGraw-Hill
Seventy-five fun and fast games and activities to warm up meetings and stimulate discussion.

Full references are provided at the end of the book.

# 4 Negotiating win-win solutions

Day in, day out, we put our negotiation skills to work – formally and informally – with clients and partners, bosses and colleagues. We use them to close sales, land a coveted promotion or job, improve communications, increase co-operation or acquire more resources.

Ideally at the end of a negotiation, everyone is happy with the outcome and able to move forward with a positive frame of mind. But how do we achieve such a happy state of affairs? Some negotiations stall or, worse still, never get off the ground.

In this theme, you will:

◆ **Identify the purpose and possible outcomes of the negotiation process**

◆ **Consider the difference between two techniques used by skilled negotiators: positional bargaining and principled negotiation**

◆ **Explore and practise the skills and techniques you need to be a successful negotiator.**

## What is negotiation?

Like it or not you are a negotiator. Negotiation is a fact of life.

Source: *Fisher, Ury and Patton* (1991)

It is easy to think that negotiation is something that happens in highly formal, specialised contexts – in particular, between unions and employers or in complex contract negotiations. However, as the above lines (which open one of the most influential books on negotiation skills) highlight, in practice all managers must be negotiators. As Fisher, Ury and Patton go on to argue: 'everyone negotiates something every day' and 'people negotiate even when they don't think of themselves as doing so'.

Fisher, Ury and Patton define negotiation as follows:

Negotiation is a basic means of getting what you want from others. It is back-and-forth communication designed to reach an agreement when you and the other side have some interests that are shared and others that are opposed.

Source: *Fisher, Ury and Patton* (1991)

Put like this, it is clear that managers have always had to negotiate in order to achieve their objectives. However, there are a number of reasons why negotiation is even more important today:

♦ The increased pace of change in modern organisations increases the need for negotiation skills. Where a programme of work may once have been set in stone for a period of time (remember the 'five-year plan'?), it is now much more likely that last month's priorities will be superseded by new challenges.

♦ The new partnerships between customer and supplier organisations have also increased the complexity of negotiation. As Rosabeth Moss Kanter (1989) argues in *When Giants Learn to Dance*, 'the supplier-customer partnership...has necessitated a more collaborative web of interfunctional relationships', both between managers in partner organisations and within the organisations themselves.

♦ At the same time, relationships within organisations have changed significantly. As Fisher, Ury and Patton (1991) argue: 'Everyone wants to participate in decisions that affect them; fewer and fewer people will accept decisions dictated to them by someone else.' In other words, negotiation now lies at the heart of working relationships.

♦ The drive for quality is another key factor here. Richard Schonberger (1990) argues that organisations can only achieve major gains in quality when 'throughout the organisation, people own and manage their processes'. Increased need for negotiation skills is central here.

## When do we negotiate?

As a manager, you negotiate in many different contexts. Here are some of the most important examples:

♦ When agreeing and prioritising workloads with members of your team you are involved in complex negotiations. You need to make sure that work is done to customer requirements; at the same time you need to ensure that individual members of the team are happy with their workloads and not working under undue stress, and that work is spread on an equitable basis throughout the team. Your skills in these negotiations are crucial both to the effectiveness and to the quality of the working atmosphere of your team.

♦ When discussing your work with your line manager, you are also likely to become involved in negotiation – whether in a formal context such as performance appraisal or in the less formal, ongoing meetings you hold. Once again, your skills here are crucial both for ensuring that your own workload is manageable and your work interesting, and for maintaining the relationship between you and your manager.

♦ When agreeing the budget for your team's activities, you may be negotiating with other managers, your own manager and other senior people. You may be competing for scarce resources and this involves another skilful balancing act to ensure that the organisation can achieve its objectives, your team has the resources it needs and other teams can carry out their own work.

♦ When planning and managing projects, you need to negotiate budgets, schedules, outcomes and so forth. These are just some of the more major negotiating landmarks in a manager's diary. You will also be involved in a multitude of other smaller negotiations, from who makes the coffee through to how people's holidays fit together. In all these negotiations, you need a clear view of possible outcomes.

## The outcomes of negotiation

When concluding any negotiation, it is vital to take a broad, long-term view of outcomes. It can be easy to embark on negotiation in a blinkered way, focusing solely on your own objectives, determined to achieve what you want at any cost.

Such an approach can be characterised as a win-lose mentality – one side in the negotiation will benefit at the expense of the other. It's 'winner takes all'.

However, this approach can easily lead to a lose-lose outcome. In the short term, both sides lose if neither is prepared to budge, and they fight themselves into the ground; in the long term, relationships suffer as people find it harder to trust each other.

All this suggests that in any negotiation, you need to balance two key factors:

♦ your own objectives – what you want to achieve from the negotiation

♦ your relationship with the other person or people involved – how you want to be able to work together in the future.

An awareness of these two factors can lead to a different approach to negotiation, one where both sides gain – a win-win outcome.

Maureen Guirdham summarises the impact that such an approach can have on negotiations:

> Negotiators are not, therefore, usually aiming to beat an opponent or extract an exploitative deal: they want one that satisfies their requirements and serves their interests.

Source: *Guirdham* (1995)

Stephen Covey (1992) argues that 'the habit of effective interpersonal leadership is Think Win/Win'. For Covey, win-win is not a technique; it is 'a total philosophy of human interaction'.

> In the long run, if it isn't a win for both of us, we both lose.
>
> Source: *Covey* (1992)

**Covey's six paradigms of interaction**

Stephen Covey argues that win-win is just one of six 'paradigms' of interaction. They are:

◆ win-win: 'a frame of mind and heart that constantly seeks mutual benefit in all human interactions'

◆ win-lose: the 'authoritarian' approach that says 'I get my way, you don't get yours'

◆ lose-win: the search for the quiet life where you finish up 'giving in or giving up'

◆ lose-lose: an approach that suggests that if no one wins, at least no one loses

◆ win: an approach based on securing your own ends and 'leaving it to others to secure theirs'

◆ win-win or no deal: Covey argues that an extension of the win-win approach is that 'if we can't agree a solution that would benefit us both, we agree to disagree agreeably'.

Source: *Covey* (1992)

Covey suggests that our choice of paradigm is partly dependent on the balance we strike between the courage of our convictions and our consideration for other people. He shows this balance in Figure 4.1

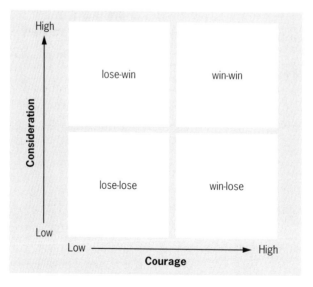

**Figure 4.1** *Paradigms of interaction*          Source: *Covey* (1992)

## Two approaches to negotiation

In the 1970s, negotiations between unions and employers were regular front-page news. The unions would put forward demands – for improved wages, better conditions of service, pension rights or involvement in decision making. The employers would make an offer – of a smaller wage increase, a pay rise spread over two or three years, or bonuses linked to productivity gains. Over a period of weeks or months the two sides would make 'improved offers' (each often called their 'final offer') until a compromise was reached or the process broke down and led to industrial action. The whole process was often acrimonious, and conducted in an adversarial climate under the threat of strikes and lay-offs.

> **All negotiators are people, with their own feelings, emotions, backgrounds and values.**

The two sides were following the time-honoured tradition of positional bargaining.

Fisher, Ury and Patton (1991) describe an alternative to positional bargaining, one that they call 'principled negotiation'.

Principled negotiation centres on the search for a mutually beneficial result – what Stephen Covey (1992) calls a 'win-win' outcome. That is not to say that everyone gets everything they want to achieve out of the negotiation – however all involved feel that the outcome is fair and, equally important, that the process of getting there has been constructive.

This section explores positional bargaining and principled negotiation in more detail.

### Positional bargaining

In this model of positional negotiation the following happens.

Each side begins by stating their position – what they claim they want to achieve from negotiation. This initial position may in fact be more than they expect to get in the end. As Maureen Guirdham (1995) argues, 'your opening offer should be pitched well away from where you expect to settle or what you would be satisfied with'. So a manager might argue that it will take eight weeks to complete a project when they know it may be possible to do it in six weeks if all goes well.

The two sides then bargain on the basis of their positions. They explain what they want and why, looking for arguments that they think may be appealing to the other side. As Guirdham argues, 'each side is always probing to find out more about the target and the resistant point of the other party, while trying to keep its own objectives concealed'. So, the manager may stress the benefits of using an experienced team throughout the project.

During the process, the positions may change. Indeed, it is common for both sides to adopt a series of positions as they make compromises or new demands. The manager might suggest that they could do the project in seven weeks if another person is brought in. Eventually, in most cases a compromise is reached. Both sides give a little and accept that getting something out of the process is better than the whole thing breaking down. The manager may have to settle for a six-week schedule.

### Uses and limitations of positional bargaining

There are clear benefits from positional bargaining. Each side states very clearly what they want to achieve so that the other side knows what is on offer. These positions give both sides a clear handle on what is being discussed. The rules are clearly laid down and accepted by both sides. Very often, positional bargaining leads, eventually, to agreement.

However, there are problems with positional bargaining. The agreement often leaves a bad taste in the mouth and can create antagonism between people who have to work together. Fisher, Ury and Patton (1991) highlight three particular risks of this approach to negotiation:

◆ Arguing over positions produces unwise agreements. People become increasingly committed to their positions at the expense of finding an agreement that is in their best interests.

◆ Arguing over positions is inefficient. There is a temptation to hold out for your own position or to make minor concessions to keep the negotiation going. A lot of time, effort and cost can go into the process.

◆ Arguing over positions endangers an ongoing relationship. Positional bargaining strains and sometimes shatters the relationship between the parties – whether at work, in social life or between partners.

So, while positional bargaining may regularly lead to agreement, this may not actually be the best agreement and may damage the working relationship. In the earlier example, the manager who finally agreed to a six-week project ended up feeling disappointed by the outcome and is highly likely to resist any further changes to the project.

## Principled negotiation

Fisher, Ury and Patton (1991) argue that principled negotiation can be boiled down to four basic points:

◆ Separate the people from the problem. All negotiators are people, with their own feelings, emotions, backgrounds and values. If you ignore these in negotiation, people's egos can get tied to their positions and there is the risk that someone will lose face. It is important to avoid this and to seek a climate of collaboration where 'participants come to see themselves as working side by side, attacking the problem, not each other'. Assertiveness skills (see Theme 2) are important here.

♦ Focus on interests, not positions. Central to the idea of principled negotiation is trying to get at the interests behind people's positions. 'Behind opposed positions lie shared and compatible interests, as well as conflicting ones.' Focusing on interests can reduce the differences between the sides and make the problem more manageable.

♦ Invent options for mutual gain. If you try to imagine a number of possible outcomes, this can increase creativity and reduce the pressure on the negotiation.

♦ Insist on using objective criteria. Finally, when weighing up the options, it makes sense to use criteria that are based on a fair standard, such as expert opinion, market value or custom. If you can agree on such criteria, you are more likely to reach agreement without one side having to back down or lose face.

**Covey's four steps to win-win solutions**
First, see the problem from the other point of view. Really seek to understand and to give expression to the needs and concerns of the other party as well as, or better than, they can themselves.

Second, identify the key issues and concerns (not positions) involved.

Third, determine what results would constitute a fully acceptable solution.

And fourth, identify possible options to achieve those results.

Source: *Covey* (1992)

## Activity 14
## Identify examples of negotiation in practice

### Objective

This activity will help you to:

◆ identify examples of negotiation in practice

◆ identify the approaches used by the negotiators.

### Task

1 Think back over the last few weeks and identify examples of negotiations that you were involved in or that affected you. These could be major negotiations, such as a new project, or smaller negotiations such as deciding where to go in the evening. Identify five or six examples and note these in the grid provided.

2 What approach to negotiation – positional bargaining or principled negotiation – was adopted? If different people used different approaches, note this down.

3 What was the outcome of the negotiation? Was it:

◆ win-win?

◆ win-lose?

◆ lose-lose?

4 In light of this, what do you see as the benefits of different approaches to bargaining? Note your conclusions in the grid.

| Negotiation | Approach(es) adopted | Outcome |
|---|---|---|
| 1 | | |
| 2 | | |
| 3 | | |
| 4 | | |
| 5 | | |
| 6 | | |
| Your conclusions: | | |

## Skills for negotiation

Negotiation starts with the assumption that there will be an agreement – all the talk is about the terms.

Source: *Guirdham* (1995)

As Maureen Guirdham (1995) argues, 'a negotiation is one type of business meeting' and, as such, many of the skills needed for preparing for, participating in and leading meetings are relevant to negotiation. In particular, the skills of ensuring that everyone gets to participate and sticking to timescales are equally relevant to a negotiation meeting. It is also vital to prepare well and to follow up any actions agreed at the end, such as producing a record of the outcomes.

Communication skills are also crucial to negotiation – Fisher, Ury and Patton (1991) highlight the importance of active listening, speaking clearly and asking appropriate questions. Techniques for assertive behaviour are clearly also vital.

However, there are some additional skills that are especially relevant to negotiation, and this section focuses on these.

## Different approaches demand different skills

It is important to recognise that positional bargaining and principled negotiation call, in some cases, for different skills. Consider the following descriptions of the process; firstly, from Maureen Guirdham describing the skills of **positional bargaining**:

Since each side is trying to attach maximum credibility to the assertion that its latest stated offer is the final one, negotiation involves rivalry in the process as well as over the issues.

Source: *Guirdham* (1995)

Compare this with Fisher, Ury and Patton who suggest that the parties involved in **principled negotiation** should see themselves:

...as partners in a hard-headed, side-by-side search for a fair agreement advantageous to each.

Source: *Fisher, Ury, and Patton* (1991)

The skills of positional bargaining are therefore based around the basic rules of the process – keeping your own cards close to your chest and looking for chinks in the other side's armour before eventually reaching an agreement.

> **The skills of positional bargaining**
> Maureen Guirdham (1995) highlights the following skills of positional bargaining:
>
> ◆ Preplanning – in particular identifying your targets, what you would like to settle for, and your resistance points, the worst position you would accept.
>
> ◆ Stating your opening position – in particular the skill of 'setting your opening offer high enough to allow you to make concessions'.
>
> ◆ Rejecting the other side's position – Guirdham argues that 'it will usually make sense to reject the opening offer, no matter how excellent a deal it seems'.
>
> ◆ Making concessions – for Guirdham, the art here is in judging the timing, when to make a concession, and in judging the size, how much to concede. You should state your concession 'with the minimum of argument, as simply as possible, in a tone of finality and in an impassive demeanour'.
>
> ◆ Encouraging movement – ways of prompting the other side into concessions in their turn by stressing your own reasonable approach and highlighting the weaknesses in their position.
>
> ◆ Getting closure – recognising when a deal is close and encouraging a conclusion.

It will also be important to formalise the agreement – if one is reached – or plan next steps if the negotiation breaks down.

By contrast, the skills of principled negotiation place much greater emphasis on openness, trust and getting to know the other side's interests, fears and concerns.

> **The skills of principled negotiation**
> Fisher, Ury and Patton (1991) describe a range of skills of principled negotiation. These include:
>
> ◆ Self-awareness and perception – questioning your own assumptions about the other side, and being able to put yourself in their shoes
>
> ◆ Handling emotions – allowing other people to let off steam without reacting aggressively or negatively towards them

- Building a working relationship – finding ways to build trust and confidence in each other and avoid blaming the other side for problems

- Identifying interests – being open about your own interests, discovering the other side's interests by asking them why they adopt their positions, uncovering shared interests and 'dovetailing' different interests

- Creativity – in particular, brainstorming possibilities, which you might ideally carry out with the other side

- Identifying fair standards and processes for conducting and concluding the negotiation.

## Developing skills

As a manager you will need to decide which approach to negotiation you wish to adopt, and to develop the skills relevant to this approach. We describe here three specific techniques that you may like to practise, which could be relevant to a wide range of work contexts.

### Practise brainstorming

Brainstorming is valuable in any situation when you need to think creatively or come up with original and alternative ideas. Brainstorming is often done in a group but can also work for the individual. With a group, however, one person's contribution may spark another's idea and so there is a richer and deeper resource for ideas.

There are four ground rules for brainstorming:

- Criticism of any ideas is not allowed until the ideas session is over

- All ideas must be acknowledged and considered, no matter how irrelevant or ridiculous they seem

- The more ideas generated the better

- Combining and refining ideas is desirable – people should draw on and develop each others' ideas.

### Know your BATNA

Your BATNA is your 'best alternative to a negotiated agreement'. Maureen Guirdham (1995) explains that your BATNA will help you to identify your resistance point – the worst point you are prepared to accept. For Fisher, Ury and Patton (1991), your BATNA is 'the standard against which any proposed agreement should be measured'. As an example, you might be negotiating for a project with a client. Your BATNA might be the lowest fee you are prepared to accept for the work.

It makes sense in any negotiation to be clear about your BATNA. What else could you do if you fail to negotiate an agreement?

## Use the circle chart

One of the main difficulties in negotiation is getting bogged down in problems. The circle chart is one way of moving beyond these by shifting your attention between the real world and what you might do in theory.

Figure 4.2 shows how it is possible to move round the circle chart between, on the one hand, what is wrong and what might be done and, on the other hand, in the real world and in theory.

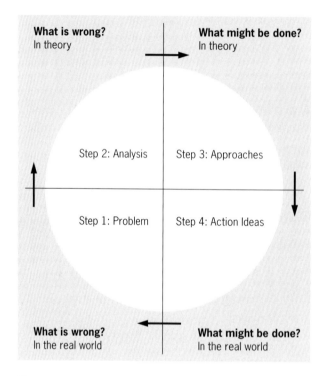

**Figure 4.2** *The circle chart*

Step 1 involves identifying what is currently wrong in the real world. Step 2 involves stepping into theory and looking at possible causes of the problem. Step 3, still at the level of theory, is about generating some broad ideas about what you could do. Step 4 involves stepping back into the real world and identifying specific practical steps to tackle the problem.

## Activity 15
### Practise using negotiation techniques

## Objective

Use this activity to practise using the circle chart to identify ways to help you around a problem.

## Task

1 Starting in the real world, identify what is currently wrong.

*Step 1*

2 Move into the realm of theory and try to identify possible causes of the problem.

*Step 2*

3 Still in theory, aim to generate some broad ideas about what you could do. You could use brainstorming as one technique here.

*Step 3*

4 Move back into the real world and identify some specific practical steps to tackle the problem.

*Step 4*

# ◆ Recap

**Identify the purpose and possible outcomes of the negotiation process**

- ◆ Negotiation is a communication process designed to reach an agreement between two parties who have some competing interests.

- ◆ The most successful outcome of a negotiation is win-win, where the solution serves the needs and interests of both parties.

- ◆ Preparing your BATNA (best alternative to a negotiated agreement) in advance will help you to recognise when you should walk away from a negotiation.

**Consider the difference between two techniques used by skilled negotiators: positional bargaining and principled negotiation**

- ◆ Positional bargaining involves each side stating their opening position (what they want to achieve) and then bargaining slowly, by making demands and concessions, to reach a new position on which both can agree.

- ◆ Principled negotiation centres on working openly to find a mutually beneficial result. The four principles are: separate the people from the problem; focus on interests rather than positions; invent a variety of options for mutual gain; and insist that the agreement be based on objective criteria.

**Explore and practise the skills and techniques you need to be a successful negotiator**

- ◆ Positional bargaining requires negotiators to be skilled in preplanning, stating their opening position, rejecting the other side's position, making concessions, encouraging movement and getting closure.

- ◆ Principled negotiation requires negotiators to possess skills of self-awareness and perception, managing emotions, building working relationships based on trust, identifying interests, creativity in developing solutions and fairness in terms of conducting and concluding the negotiation.

 **More @**

**Fisher, R., Ury, W. and Patton, B. (2003)** *Getting to Yes,* **Random House Business Books**
This is an updated version of their original text on principled negotiation.

**Ghauri, P. and Usunier, J-C. (2003) 2nd edition,** *International Business Negotiations*, **Pergamon**
Explore the impact of culture and communication on international business negotiations.

**McCann, D. (2004)** *How to Influence Others at Work,* **Butterworth-Heinemann**
Develop your communication skills so that you are able to influence the outcome of conversations. See also **www.tms.com.au/influencing.html**

Full references are provided at the end of the book.

# 5 Recognising and managing conflict

Conflict is a frequent event in managers' lives. You might find yourself arbitrating a conflict between two people you manage. You might be in disagreement yourself with a colleague who thinks differently from you or who is fighting for the same resources. You might inadvertently exacerbate existing conflicts, either by being unaware of them or by jumping to conclusions too quickly.

People react very differently to conflict. Stop and think for a minute about your own response. Do you battle the issues head on? Do you negotiate a compromise or do you prefer to avoid conflict altogether?

Although we have natural preferences, we are all capable of using a range of styles and no particular response is correct every time. The more aware you are of your personal style and the more ways you can see of resolving a particular conflict, the more considerate and successful you will be in solving the problem.

In this theme, you will:

♦ **Identify sources of conflict and enhance your ability to recognise conflicts and disagreements at work**

♦ **Examine the role of the manager in managing conflict so that it does not become damaging to the individual or organisations involved**

♦ **Reflect on the range of strategies that you use to deal with conflict and consider how you can develop these further.**

## Why does conflict happen?

Interpersonal conflict occurs between two or more persons when attitudes, motives, values, expectations or activities are incompatible and if those people perceive themselves to be in disagreement.

Source: *Hunt* (1982)

Few organisations are immune to conflict – indeed Fisher, Ury and Patton (1991) comment that 'conflict is a growth industry'. Conflict may happen between individuals within a team; it may break out between teams; it may permeate the whole climate of the organisation.

There are many potential causes of conflict:

♦ Conflicts often occur over power and interest – as a result of one group or individual protecting their own interests or intruding on someone else's interests

♦ Conflicts can also stem from clashes of personality – between people who find it hard to get on

♦ Conflicts can arise when people have contrasting values and beliefs – different ideas about how things should be done

♦ Rapid change or organisational restructuring often increases the level of conflict.

Leading writers on conflict in organisations are Kakabadse, Ludlow and Vinnicombe. In *Working in Organisations* (1987), they comment that:

> In all organisations, individuals compete for resources, for attention, for influence; there are differences of opinion as to the priorities and objectives to be attained; clashes of values and beliefs occur frequently.

Source: *Kakabadse et al.* (1987)

**Five reasons for differences in organisations**
Andrew Kakabadse (1983) highlights five reasons why conflicts arise:

♦ **Grand strategy versus local identity:** changes that result from the organisation's senior managers – such as new products, new technologies or plant closures – disrupt the working of local teams

♦ **Superiors versus subordinates:** tensions can also occur between levels of hierarchy over salary, status, authority and respect

♦ **Management versus operatives:** there can be particular tensions between managers and shop-floor workers – differences in cultures, attitudes and commitment to the organisation

♦ **Professional versus administrator:** within an organisation, some people may hold dual allegiances – in particular, professional and specialist staff may encounter conflict between their professional values and those of the organisation

♦ **Planning versus execution:** different departments – for example, design and manufacturing, or marketing and production – may have different priorities.

In certain contexts more than one of these may be at work.

Source: *Kakabadse* (1983)

# Conflict in teams

Given the scope for conflict within organisations, it is not surprising that problems can erupt at team level. There are two key aspects of conflict that are likely to concern an individual manager:

**Conflict within the team** – there may be conflict between individual team members, or between the team and the manager. Such conflict may stem from:

◆ confusion over roles, when people are unsure who should be doing what

◆ conflicts of priorities, where different people feel their work is more important

◆ conflict over ways of doing things

◆ personality clashes.

**Conflict between teams** – there may also be tension between one team and another. Charles Handy (1993) suggests that such conflicts stem from two underlying causes:

◆ objectives and ideologies – where different teams have divergent objectives, overlapping roles or different views about what they should do

◆ territory and roles – where one team intrudes on another's jealously guarded patch.

# Constructive and destructive conflict

Conflict is not always a bad thing, however. Maureen Guirdham (1995) argues that we can distinguish between constructive and destructive conflict.

Constructive conflict:

> ...can lead to more creative solutions to problems, and can force people to tackle the socio-emotional issues, so clearing the air for more concentrated attention on tasks.
>
> Source: *Guirdham* (1995)

However, as Guirdham comments, 'drawing a line between constructive and destructive conflict is not always easy'.

**Four signs that conflict is becoming destructive**

Maureen Guirdham highlights four signs that conflict may be becoming destructive:

♦ There is a threat of a whole organisation or group disintegrating or splitting into camps

♦ The organisation or group's goals are being subverted by the conflict

♦ An individual is being attacked persistently

♦ The conflict goes on too long.

**Conflict can be very disturbing to some people's self-esteem and sense of identity.**

Source: *Guirdham* (1995)

# Activity 16
## Keep a conflict log

### Objective

Use this activity to increase your awareness of conflict. It will help you to keep a log of conflict.

### Task

Over the next month, keep a record of any conflicts that affect you in some way. Use the log provided to keep your record.

1  Describe what happened, including who was involved.

2  Analyse the possible causes of conflict. Was the conflict caused by a clash of values or beliefs? Was it a conflict over power or interest? Were personal antagonisms involved or organisational changes to blame?

3  Describe how the people affected sought to tackle it. How effective were their attempts to solve the problem? Were they able to steer the conflict towards a constructive outcome, or did they make matters worse?

4  Note down what you have learned from your experiences of conflict about:

♦ ways in which you can create an atmosphere of openness and trust

♦ ways in which you can move conflict towards a constructive outcome.

| What happened | Why this happened | What you did |
|---|---|---|
| 1 | | |
| 2 | | |
| 3 | | |
| 4 | | |
| 5 | | |
| 6 | | |

What you have learned:

## The role of the manager

Given the frequency and importance of conflict in organisations, managers clearly have an important role to play in reducing its destructive effects.

There are several aspects to your role. You need to:

♦ recognise the symptoms of conflict

♦ recognise your own style for dealing with conflict

♦ adopt appropriate strategies for resolving conflict

♦ work with organisational procedures for conflict management.

> **Confronting the difficult issues is not easy – but it may be necessary**

### Recognising the symptoms of conflict

In some cases, conflict is open and explicit. Members of your team may come to you about a problem or you may witness people arguing over an issue.

However, this is not always the case. Conflict often simmers away without ever breaking the surface. Such hidden conflict is often more damaging than open conflict – it can fester for long periods, getting in the way of the work that people are doing and damaging the climate within the team.

You need to be able to recognise the symptoms of hidden conflict so that you can decide what to do about it. Such symptoms could include:

◆ a deteriorating atmosphere

◆ people making unpleasant snipes and comments about colleagues or other teams

◆ people avoiding each other or refusing to talk to each other

◆ an increase in the number of memos or e-mails flying round the office

◆ an 'us and them' attitude towards other parts of the organisation.

It is vital to recognise such symptoms and to get to the bottom of them quickly. As Charles Handy argues, though, it is important to tackle the cause of the problem, rather than the symptoms themselves:

> The strategy for resolving conflict must be related to the disease, not the symptom. Diagnosis, therefore, differentiating between symptoms and cause, is the key to proper management of conflict.

Source: *Handy* (1993)

**Charles Handy: Six symptoms of conflict**
Charles Handy identifies six symptoms of organisational conflict, as follows:

1 Poor communications – where decisions are taken on the basis of the wrong information.

2 Inter-group hostility and jealousy – when people comment that 'they never tell us anything' or 'they seem totally unaware'.

3 Inter-personal friction – where relationships deteriorate or people stop talking to each other.

4 Escalation of arbitration – where disputes get referred up the hierarchy.

5 Proliferation of rules and regulations, norms and myths – if things get more formal and pedantic, this may also be a symptom of conflict.

6 Low morale – where people find it hard to feel positive about their work.

Source: *Handy* (1993)

So, you need to look behind the symptoms and examine what may be causing the problems.

## Styles of dealing with conflict

It is also important to recognise that we all react to conflict in different ways depending on the context, the people involved and our own personal styles.

Thomas (1976) has researched managers' personal styles of dealing with conflict. He argues that it is possible to classify conflict-handling styles depending on the importance you place on your:

◆ concern with your own needs

◆ concern with others' needs.

**K W Thomas: Five conflict-handling styles**
Thomas has identified five different styles for handling conflict, as shown in Figure 5.1:

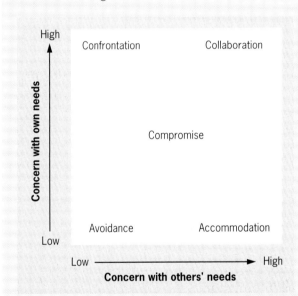

**Figure 5.1** *Conflict-handling styles*          Source: *Thomas* (1976)

◆ Confrontation involves up-front responses, such as demanding an apology, regardless of who really caused the conflict

◆ Avoidance involves refusing to recognise that conflict exists

◆ Accommodation involves apologising and 'giving in', again regardless of the real causes of the problem

◆ Compromise involves bargaining to achieve an acceptable outcome

◆ Collaboration involves working with the other people to try to solve the problem.

Note that the term 'confrontation' is sometimes used in a different way. Writers such as Charles Handy talk about 'confronting conflict' as a way of dealing openly with the problem. Such an approach is close to Thomas's collaborative style.

Different styles for handling conflict can all work, depending on the context and people involved. However, some are more likely to be effective than others:

- Avoidance can sometimes be an acceptable short-term strategy, but it leaves the problem untouched and will lead to more conflict in the future.

- Confrontation and accommodation have much in common with the aggressive and submissive behaviours described in Theme 2 on assertiveness. Again, they may resolve the immediate short-term problem. However, in the longer term they tend, in Maureen Guirdham's words, 'to reinforce the conflict and create more ill feeling, to prolong it below the surface, and to encourage further aggression in others' (Guirdham, 1995).

- Compromise is often an appropriate style to adopt. However, it has something in common with the positional bargaining described in Theme 4 – there is a risk that the compromise achieved does not best serve the interests of those involved.

- Collaboration can be a challenging style to adopt, and demands significant time and personal commitment. To quote Maureen Guirdham again: 'It is clear that this is usually the best approach.' However, dealing openly and collaboratively with conflict is not easy for everyone. The remainder of this section looks at how you can adopt a collaborative approach to conflict resolution, and at some practical techniques you can use to deal with conflict – and indeed encourage your team to use as well.

## Activity 17
## Examine your own strategies for dealing with conflict

### Objective

This activity will help you to examine your own strategies for dealing with conflict.

### Task

1  Consider a conflict that you were involved in. Describe it briefly here.

*Description of conflict:*

2  Which of the following approaches most reflected your reaction? Tick the appropriate box:

- ☐ Confrontation
- ☐ Avoidance
- ☐ Accommodation
- ☐ Collaboration
- ☐ Compromise

3  In tackling the problem, how important to you were each of the following:

- ◆ Concern for your own needs?

  Very important < ☐ ☐ ☐ ☐ ☐ > Not important

- ◆ Concern for others' needs?

  Very important < ☐ ☐ ☐ ☐ ☐ > Not important

**4** Does this reflect how you respond to conflict generally?

*Write your thoughts here:*

## Feedback

It is worth spending some time thinking about the consequences of each approach to conflict. How you react to conflict will send important messages to other people about how you value yourself and other people. If you are able to adopt a collaborative approach to resolving conflicts, working with the other people involved to try to solve the problems, this is most likely to lead to win-win outcomes. If you tend to adopt:

♦ a confrontation style, you may need to think of ways in which you can raise your concern with others' needs

♦ an accommodation style, you may need to think of ways in which you can raise your concern for your own needs

♦ an avoidance style, you may need to think of ways in which you can take more active steps in handling conflict

♦ a compromise style, you may like to try out a more collaborative approach.

## Strategies for resolving conflict

Here are some strategies that you can adopt to help resolve conflict:

♦ find root causes

♦ confront difficult issues

♦ raise emotional literacy.

### Find root causes

You are most likely to resolve a conflict if you know what is causing it, so you need to be able to drill down to establish the root cause or causes.

To do this you need to talk with the person or people involved. Bear in mind that people may at first present you with concerns that are not the root causes – you may need to probe to get at the real issues.

To be completely sure of the causes you need to talk to all involved – individually or together, depending on the people concerned. When you are clear about the causes, you can start to tackle them.

Some causes may be relatively easy to tackle. There may be misunderstandings to resolve, or there may be steps that you, as manager, can take to put things right – for example, by relocating tasks or giving people new responsibilities.

Other causes may be harder to tackle. If this is the case, you may need to confront the underlying issues with the people involved.

### Confront difficult issues

> Confrontation takes considerable courage, and many people would prefer to take the course of least resistance... But in the long run, people will trust and respect you more if you are honest and open and kind with them. You care enough to confront.

Source: *Covey* (1992)

As Covey points out, confronting the difficult issues is not easy – but it may be necessary. Examples of when you may need to tackle an underlying issue could include the following:

♦ someone consistently letting the team down – by arriving late or failing to complete their work without an appropriate reason

♦ someone behaving inappropriately towards other people in the team – for example, being rude or inconsiderate

♦ problems about how someone behaves towards internal or external customers or clients

♦ someone failing to work to the standards of their professional practice

♦ value problems, such as prejudice or bias.

99

Confronting issues like these does not mean getting cross with the person or people involved. It involves talking the issue through with them and giving them feedback about their behaviour. It helps if you follow the rules for constructive feedback:

◆ Focus on the behaviour rather than the person. Avoid personalising the issue (for example, by saying 'you're a difficult person') and instead highlight what they did (for example, 'I found what you said hurtful').

◆ Describe the behaviour rather than judging it. Try to avoid saying things like, 'that was a terrible thing to do'.

◆ Give specific examples; for example, 'you were late for the last two team meetings' rather than 'you are always late'.

◆ Seek the other person's explanation. They have the right to put their point of view, and it is vital to find out whether you both see the problem the same way.

◆ Look beneath the surface. It is quite possible that there are other reasons for the problem – for example, in the person's private life.

◆ Look for alternative ways forward. You need to move on from the problem and to find solutions. If you consider alternatives, this gives the other person choice.

Two sets of skills are highly relevant here:

◆ Some of the techniques for assertiveness are especially relevant to conflict – in particular, it is helpful to focus on the rights of the people involved.

◆ The skills of principled negotiation are helpful for identifying interests and finding workable solutions.

### Raise emotional literacy

In the longer term, you can best tackle conflict in the team by ensuring that everyone in the team is, in David Goleman's words, 'emotionally literate'. Goleman (1995) argues that the most important emotional skills include:

◆ self-awareness

◆ identifying, expressing and managing feelings

◆ controlling impulses to act on the spur of the moment

◆ handling stress and anxiety.

## Techniques for tackling problems

You and your team may find a number of other techniques helpful for tackling problems, in particular:

◆ techniques of transactional analysis

◆ positioning exercises

◆ estrangement exercises.

## Transactional analysis

Transactional analysis (TA), described earlier in this book, is highly relevant to conflict.

> In team contexts, the Adult, Nurturing Parent and Natural Child states can be most helpful. The Critical Parent and Adapted Child can be destructive. If members of a team become aware of these ideas, they can refer to them at appropriate moments – for example, 'This is your Parent talking'.

Source: *Berne* (1968)

## Positioning exercises

Positioning exercises are drawn from the ideas of neuro-linguistic programming (NLP). These exercises are designed to help people step into each other's shoes. They involve imagining the interaction from two or three different perspectives:

◆ The first position is your own point of view.

◆ The second position is the point of view of the other person – this involves seeking to understand the world from their perspective.

◆ The third position is the point of view of an observer – this involves looking at the interaction from a more detached perspective.

As with TA, it can be valuable for team members to learn this technique so that they can use it at appropriate points – for instance, where there is potential conflict within the group or for dealing with a difficult colleague.

## Estrangement exercises

Hawkins and Shohet (1998) describe 'estrangement exercises' – you could use this technique to examine how your team is functioning and identify possible sources of conflict. To do this you ask an individual or individuals in your team to take some time to mentally 'step back' out of the group so that they can observe group processes from the perspective of an external observer. They then seek to identify and feed back to the group:

◆ what the group is doing well and should build on

◆ what the group is not doing well and should change

◆ the one main issue they would like the group to address.

Source: *Hawkins and Shohet* (1998)

## Organisational procedures

Organisations also have mechanisms for managing conflict, in particular discipline and grievance procedures. Charles Handy (1993) highlights other mechanisms found in some organisations, including:

◆ rules and regulations designed to get round the problem – for example, setting up a system for handover of a piece of work between one section and another

◆ arbitration to resolve conflict between teams and individuals

◆ creating a post in the organisation with responsibility to liaise between conflicting teams

◆ separating conflicting groups or individuals.

## Activity 18
## Practise techniques for tackling conflict issues

### Objective

Use this activity to practise techniques for tackling conflict issues. To tackle an episode of conflict, you need to:

◆ find root causes

◆ confront difficult issues.

### Task

Use the numbered boxes in the grid to note down your answers.

1 Identify an episode of conflict that is affecting you at the moment. You could focus on your own relationship with another person or relationships within your team.

2 Note down what you think the root causes of the problem may be.

3 Arrange to talk to the other person(s) involved. What are their perceptions about the conflict and the reasons for it?

4 How might you go about resolving the problem? Bear in mind the techniques described earlier. Note down what you propose to do.

5 Record what actually happens.

6 What have you learned about conflict from this?

| 1 Briefly describe the problem | 2 Root causes |
|---|---|
| | |

| 3 Perceptions about conflict | 4 Proposal |
|---|---|
| | |

| 5 What actually happens | 6 What you have learned |
|---|---|
| | |

# ◆ Recap

**Identify sources of conflict and enhance your ability to recognise conflicts and disagreements at work**

- ◆ Individuals, teams and departments can be in conflict with each other due to misuse of power, poor communication, clashes of personality, differing values, differing approaches to doing things and incompatible goals and priorities.

- ◆ Constructive conflict can force people out of comfort zones, lead to creative solutions and improve organisational performance. Destructive conflict can be disturbing to people's self-esteem and motivation, lowering individual and organisational performance.

103

**Examine the role of the manager in managing conflict so that it does not become damaging to the individual or organisations involved**

- The five styles for managing conflict are avoidance, compromise, accommodation, competitive/confrontational and collaborative.

- The collaborative approach to handling conflict is preferable but the different styles can all work, depending on the context and people involved.

**Reflect on the range of strategies that you use to deal with conflict and consider how you can develop these further**

- To resolve a conflict you need first to understand what is causing it. Transactional analysis, positioning and estrangement exercises are all tools that help you to see the issues from the perspective of the other person or people involved.

- When confronting someone about an issue, follow the rules for constructive feedback to put across your point of view. Focus on understanding the other person's interests and on generating a range of solutions to resolve the conflict.

 **More @**

Covey, S. (2000) *The Seven Habits of Highly Successful People: Powerful Lessons for Personal Change*, Sagebrush Education Resources
This is a hugely popular text for developing your personal and professional effectiveness.

Goleman, D. (2000), *Working With Emotional Intelligence*, Bantam
Explore how to manage conflict by becoming emotionally literate. See also www.eiconsortium.org/index.html

Handy, C. (1993) *Understanding Organisations*, Penguin Business

www.kilmann.com/conflict.html for more on the Thomas-Kilmann conflict mode inventory.

Full references are provided at the end of the book.

# References

Adair, J. (1997) *Effective communication: the most important management tool of all*, Pan

Adair, J. (1983) *Effective Leadership*, Gower

Alberti, R. E. and Emmons, M. L. (1978) *Your Perfect Right*, Impact.

Back, K. and Back, K. (1999) *Assertiveness at Work*, McGraw-Hill.

Barker, A. (1997) *How to Hold Better Meetings*, Kogan Page

Barker, A. (2000) *Improve Your Communication Skills*, Kogan Page.

Barlow, J. et al. (2002) 1st edition, *Smart Videoconferencing: New Habits for Virtual Meetings*, Berrett-Koehler Publishers Inc.

Berne, E. (1968) *Games People Play*, Penguin

Boisot, M. (1987) *Information in Organisations: The Manager as Anthropologist*, Fontana

Caunt, J. (2000) *Organise Yourself*, Kogan Page

Covey, S. R. (1992) *The Seven Habits of Highly Effective People*, Simon & Schuster

Dickson, A. (2000) *Women at Work*, Kogan Page

Fayol, H. (1916) *General and Industrial Administration*, Dunod

Fisher, R., Ury, W. and Patton, B. (1991) *Getting to Yes*, Century

Fleming, I. (1997) 4th edition, *The Time Management Pocketbook*, Management Pocketbooks Ltd

Gillen, T. (1992*) Assertiveness for Managers*, Gower

Goleman, D. (2000) *Working With Emotional Intelligence*, Bantam

Guirdham, M. (1995) *Interpersonal Skills at Work*, Prentice Hall

Handy, C. (1993) *Understanding Organisations*, Penguin Business

Harris, T. (1995) *I'm OK – You're OK*, Arrow

Hawkins, P. and Shohet, R. (1998) *Supervision in the Helping Professions*, Open University Press

Heller, R. (1998) *Communicate Clearly*, Dorling Kindersel

The Herald (2001) 'Raising confident children', Part 3, 26 May Supplement

Hindle, T. (1998) *Managing Meetings*, Dorling Kindersely

Holland, S. and Ward, C. (1990) *Assertiveness: A Practical Approach*, Winslow

Hunt, J. (1982) *Managing People in Organisations*, McGraw-Hill

Isaacs, W. (1999) *Dialogue and the Art of Thinking Together: A Pioneering Approach to Communicating in Business and in Life,* Bantam Doubleday Dell Publishing Group

Kakabadse, A. (1983*) The Politics of Management,* Gower

Kakabadse, A., Ludlow, R. and Vinnicombe, S. (1987) *Working in Organisations,* Gower

Kanter, R. M. (1989) *When Giants Learn to Dance,* Simon & Schuster

Knasel, E., Meed, J. and Rossetti, A. (2000) *Learn for your life,* Pearson Education

Liebenau, J. and Backhouse, J. (1990) *Understanding Information,* MacMillan

Lifeskills Associates Ltd (1988) *Asssertiveness,* Lifeskills.

Lindenfield, G. (1986) *Assert Yourself,* Thorsons

Murdoch, A. and Scutt, C. (2002) 3rd edition, *Personal Effectiveness,* Butterworth-Heinemann

Newstrom, J. and Scannell, E. (1995) *Big Book of Business Games: Icebreakers, Creativity Exercises and Meeting Energizers,* McGraw-Hill

Open University (1984) *The Effective Manager,* Open University Press

Open University (1990) *Better Meetings,* Open University Press

Schonberger, R. J. (1990) *Building a Chain of Customers,* Hutchinson

Seely Brown, J. et al (2004) *Storytelling in Organizations: Why Storytelling Is Transforming 21st Century Organizations and Management,* Butterworth-Heinemann

Senge, P., Kleiner, A., Roberts, C., Ross, R. B. and Smith, B. (1994) *The Fifth Discipline Handbook,* Nicholas Brealey

Stanton, N. (1990) 2nd edition, *Communication,* The Macmillan Press

Thomas, K. W. (1976) Conflict and Conflict Management, in M. D. Dunnette (ed), *Handbook of Industrial and Organisational Psychology,* Houghton Mifflin